LIVED EXPERIENCES, CHALLENGES, AND LEARNINGS ABOUT DYSPRAXIA

Kimberley Fraser

LIVED EXPERIENCES, CHALLENGES, AND LEARNINGS ABOUT DYSPRAXIA

Toward Greater Inclusion

Disability Studies

Collection Editors

Dr Damian Mellifont
&
Dr Jennifer Smith-Merry

First published in 2024 by Lived Places Publishing

British Library Cataloguing in Publication Data
A CIP record for this book is available from the British Library

ISBN: 9781916704404 (pbk)
ISBN: 9781916704428 (ePDF)
ISBN: 9781916704411 (ePUB)

The right of Kimberley Fraser to be identified as the Author of this work have been asserted by them in accordance with the Copyright, Design and Patents Act 1988.

Cover design by Fiachra McCarthy
Book design by Rachel Trolove of Twin Trail Design
Typeset by Newgen Publishing UK

Lived Places Publishing
Long Island
New York 11789

www.livedplacespublishing.com

> If you judge a fish by its ability to climb a tree, it will live its whole life believing it is stupid.

Attributed to Albert Einstein

Obviously, fish cannot climb trees. Some things are biologically impossible. But it is a reminder that we cannot judge everybody by the same benchmarks, and everyone has their own unique strengths.

I have loved this quote ever since I first saw it as a teenager. It is now widely accepted that Einstein was neurodivergent, and almost certainly had dyspraxia (Oxford Specialist Tutors, 2018). One of my favourite dyspraxia geek facts is that Einstein was still unable to tie his shoelaces at the time of his death. But despite his disabilities, he is still widely regarded as one of the greatest minds of our time.

Abstract

This book takes the reader on a journey through the lived experiences of the author as a person with dyspraxia. Starting with early childhood and diagnosis, the author shares their wins and challenges throughout areas of education, employment, and independent living. This text challenges people to be accommodating of difference, to avoid unfair judgements, and to remain open-minded about the many attributes that can accompany neurodivergence. Attributes that include those of attention to detail, honesty, and high motivation.

This book calls for a more inclusive society and provides lessons and practical ways forward to achieve this. It raises hope for the future and sees widespread and inclusive change for people with dyspraxia happening sooner rather than later.

Keywords

Dyspraxia, disability, accommodations, inclusion, diversity, employment

Content warning

This book contains descriptions of and references to situations which may cause distress in some readers.

This book includes topics of:

- Hospitalization
- Disability discrimination
- Bullying
- Mobbing
- Micro-aggressions
- Stigma

Please be aware that the above-mentioned topics are **commonly discussed throughout the book**.

Contents

Learning objectives

This book aims to encourage readers to:

1. Understand the author's lived experiences with dyspraxia;
2. Recognize the barriers to a greater social and economic inclusion of people with dyspraxia;
3. Identify practical ways of making places (e.g. schools, higher education, workplaces) more inclusive of people with dyspraxia;
4. The risks that can accompany unauthorized disclosures of disability;
5. Understand the many attributes that can accompany neurodivergence;
6. Recognize and challenge all forms of disability discrimination.

Introduction

I have dyspraxia. Dyspraxia is frequently misdiagnosed, overlooked, or simply misunderstood. Awareness of dyspraxia's symptoms and effects have increased in recent years, thanks largely to the public profile of Harry Potter actor Daniel Radcliffe. Because dyspraxia is completely invisible and doesn't impair intelligence, it is often assumed that you are lazy, stupid, or simply not trying hard enough (O'Dea et al., 2021). I have experienced this throughout my life in education, in work, and while looking for a job. One thing that has always puzzled me about my dyspraxia is why I remember random details and past events from years ago, often in bizarre detail, like the exact address that one of my aunties lived at in 1998. Yet I find it impossible to recall what happened yesterday, what I had for breakfast that morning, or the conversation we had minutes ago.

While there are exceptions, see for example Colley (2006), much of the material that you see online or in books is focused on dyspraxia in children, particularly boys. But those children grow up. Our differences don't magically disappear when we turn 18, though typically support does. Navigating through life with an invisible difference is challenging and at times very frustrating, especially when your difficulties seem to contradict your intellect. This often leads to people assuming that you aren't disabled, which I have experienced over and over again. I have always been very keen for people to understand that while my disability has no bearing on my intelligence, it causes more challenges and chaos than people would perhaps imagine. I have had to accept that I will never do a lot of the things I wanted to do and just assumed I would, like driving.

I have wanted to write a book as far back as I can remember. But being neurodivergent and an almost textbook dyspraxic, I've never done anything about it, until now. I'm both excited and terrified by the idea. As I have already mentioned, a lot of the materials written on dyspraxia are aimed at young people and their carers or are written solely for academic purposes. I have seen little written by adults with dyspraxia, particularly concerning our own lived experiences. My lived experiences are valuable as teachers, educational establishments, authority figures, and even doctors often have less knowledge about my condition than me.

I want to challenge the commonly held belief that neurodivergence is less severe or impacts you less than a physical disability. It is not less or more, better or worse, it's simply different. This book aims to provide valuable insights into how you can understand and help people with dyspraxia as an educator, employer, or someone in the medical field. I will explain my experiences and the challenges I have faced throughout my life with my disability and try to provide a deeper understanding of what dyspraxia is, the challenges that I have faced as someone with an invisible disability, and how they could have been avoided or addressed more effectively if professionals were willing to listen to those with lived experience. And particularly those with conditions like dyspraxia, which are still lesser known and understood than other neurotypes.

In the chapters to follow, I will take you, the reader, on a journey through my early childhood experiences including my diagnosis, my primary, high school and college experiences, and my experiences with independent living. I'll then provide some important life-learnings to support a greater social and economic inclusion of people with dyspraxia, before concluding with some comments about my hopes for the future. Finally, I'll provide some suggested discussion topics that cover the book content.

1
Early childhood and diagnosis

My challenging start in this world

I was born eight weeks prematurely on 2 July 1987, weighing 3 lbs 13 oz. Although I was born prematurely I appeared otherwise healthy until I became ill through the night and was subsequently moved to the special nursery unit. I had stopped breathing and had been put on a ventilator with oxygen and a drip had to be inserted in to my head. My mum and dad weren't told any of this until the following morning. The nurse came in and casually told my mum not to be alarmed as I was now on a ventilator. She even asked if she wanted to see me immediately, or if she would like to have breakfast first! Upon meeting the doctor, they were then informed that I had somehow picked up a bug in my blood. They were told that it was something that everyone carries on their skin but that they were baffled as to why this had happened. The reason being that I had been in an incubator and in theory it shouldn't have been possible for me to pick up an infection. My parents would later find out that I had contracted septicaemia. Unbelievably, this is not something that they ever remember being specifically informed of. I had a barrage of tests, and antibiotics daily to clear the infection. For a while, I was very ill, and had blood drawn several times a day to check that the antibiotics I was given were working as they should. When I was eventually taken off the oxygen, I had to have a feeding tube inserted as at that point, I was too ill to be lifted out to be fed. I had a blood transfusion when I was less than a week old.

As a newborn, all of the clothes available for babies drowned me, and so my grandmas were kept busy, as they knitted most of my clothes. I couldn't wear standard baby clothes for months, as I was hooked up to a drip, feeding tubes, and oxygen. The drip tube was in my head, and I regularly had blood taken from my heels, to check that the antibiotics for the septicaemia were working as they should. The blood was taken from my feet as this was the easiest way to get blood from me as a newborn, because I was so small. Even now, I still have the marks on my feet. And because the doctors needed access to the equipment at all times, it was impractical to dress me in Babygros or cute twin sets. So, my Nannie fashioned a knitted dress which tied at the sides. I would eventually be taken off the ventilator and have all the tubes removed weeks later. Mum said it was the most exciting thing ever to see me in a normal hospital cot, in normal baby clothes.

Discharge from hospital

I was finally discharged from hospital the day before my due date. Just before I was discharged, my mum and dad had their first night out in months. On this particular night they bumped into the junior doctor and nurses from the hospital who were out celebrating, having finished their studies for the year. My parents recognized them from all their time spent in the hospital and they were so grateful to them for caring for me. My mum explained they felt they could never repay the doctors for the wonderful job that they did, so my parents bought them many drinks over the next few hours. This maybe wasn't such a great idea as they were due to fly out on holiday the next day, it's safe to say most likely with impressive hangovers.

The consequences of my disability going unrecognized

The earliest indication of my disability being missed did not happen until I began school as my challenges were all previously simply attributed to my premature birth. As my parents' first child, they didn't have anyone to compare me against. I don't ever remember being told that I had a disability, though it became obvious to my parents over time that I was different. As a baby I had physiotherapy as my joints were inflexible. From a very early age, I always needed to wear socks and shoes and always needed my hands to be clean. Cleaning my teeth and brushing my hair was painful and I would try to avoid these activities. Looking back, this avoidance was related to my sensory processing issues. I hated being dirty or having dirty clothes. I didn't like the feeling of sand.

I have a sister who is ten months younger than me, and she hit milestones like walking before I did. Despite this I had more advanced language skills than other children my age and could sing entire songs at two years old. I never crawled as a baby, despite my dad's ingenious idea of laying out chocolate buttons on the floor in front of me. When I eventually started walking at 18 months, it looked stilted, as if it was unnatural. I would have occupational therapy to help me at a later stage once I was in school.

I was clumsy as a child; I tripped and stumbled a lot. I have multiple scars on my hands and legs from tripping and falling over the years, and also a couple on my face. Some of these are faded line marks around my mouth, when I tripped and fell off a bench in nursery class and my teeth went through my lips and chin. Apparently, I wasn't particularly concerned about it and simply went up to the teacher and casually said that I thought something was wrong, with blood dripping off my chin. The pre-school teacher understandably had a slightly different reaction. I think I needed some paper stitches for that. The day before my seventh birthday, I had another accident, but this time it wasn't me who caused it! My sister and I were playing with a boomerang, which I found impossible to throw. My sister didn't have much more success. So, an older kid picked it up and threw it and this time it did come back – hitting me right between my eyes and above my eyebrow, needing seven paper stitches. I just walked casually into the house and, again, wasn't overly concerned about what had happened. Mum still has the photo of me with my birthday cake, black eye, stitches, and all. I am always cold, and as a child would lie directly in front of our electric fire with my feet above my head resting on the hood. I was very flexible and so this wasn't uncomfortable. I preferred being on the floor to sitting on seats anyway, I think I found it was easier for me to balance. But when I was seven years old this led to another accident, when I went to get up and fell back, my hand pressing against the hot glass. I had two bandaged fingers for a week.

Diagnosis at last!

My dyspraxia was diagnosed surprisingly late in my childhood. I had already been at school at least a few years when my symptoms became more apparent. I was always losing things and was unable to find my way around. In the 1990s my parents were told that I had "motor learning difficulties". This is, of course, now an outdated term but still better than the offensive term it replaced, which was "minimal brain damage". Though we had a name, the condition was still relatively unknown and information about my condition was hard to find.

I have vague memories of occupational therapy, and appointments with an educational psychologist, a lovely soft-spoken woman with a round, ruddy face and curly white hair. The occupational therapy was mainly focused on improving my poor hand–eye coordination and the strength in my hands. I had poor grip strength, and this affected my writing. In turn, this slowed me down and often meant I'd be rushing to write what we had been told before I forgot it, while trying to listen at the same time. My concentration would wander during the day, and I'd often be distracted or behind in my work, despite trying my hardest. I don't think that the occupational therapy I had as a child was overly beneficial. But at the time, dyspraxia was poorly understood, and I think that even doctors and teachers struggled to know how best to help me. I believe that they did their best with the limited knowledge that was available about dyspraxia at the time.

You would be forgiven for assuming that a childhood diagnosis makes the experience of disability easier. After all, you have a name for your condition and at least a very basic understanding of what it may mean for you going forward. But it also means knowing that you are different from the other kids, even if you don't yet understand why. My diagnosis coming when it did was both a blessing and a curse. It meant that teachers were slightly more inclined to be patient when I struggled, but despite a vague diagnosis, support was still difficult to find. Even when identified, there were constant delays, queries, and questions as to whether I "really needed" a high level of support as I was articulate for my age and appeared outwardly intelligent.

I always felt exposed when I couldn't do things that other children managed with ease. People in general have always seemed to struggle with the idea that you can be bright and intelligent, but yet struggle with everyday life. For many people, if you don't see the disability, they believe it "can't be that bad", which simply isn't true. I think you learn fairly quickly as a neurodivergent young person to hide the parts of your personality that other kids see as odd or weird. But it takes a long time to understand that actually you should never have had to do that in the first place in order to be accepted. In the next chapter, I'll talk about masking and other challenges relating to my primary school experiences.

2
Primary school experiences

Realization of difference in primary school settings

I don't remember at exactly what age I realized that I was different from other kids. My issues with short-term memory loss wouldn't become apparent until I was in school, but this has been one of the defining and most challenging aspects of my disability. By the time I was well into primary school I was beginning to grasp that I struggled with things that other kids didn't need to think about. Although early on in primary school my teachers were beginning to suspect I was experiencing difficulties, but I don't think I really noticed that I was any different from my friends.

In primary school, I discovered that I often lost things, that I really didn't understand maths, and that I couldn't really concentrate for long periods. But to me this was normal. Still, I did pick up on routines and remembered to follow them. Though I found it really difficult to get used to anything new, it was always accepted that was simply the way I was. Supporting this status quo, my parents had been told all the issues that were beginning to appear were just simply a result of my premature birth and I would always take longer to grasp new things.

I think I knew on some level that I didn't function in the same way as other kids. But as a young child you can't articulate this fact. My disability wouldn't cause as much anguish as it would later as I had friends I had grown up with, and they simply accepted that I forgot lots of things. They would tie my shoelaces for me, help me zip up my jacket, and drag me along to class to make sure that I didn't get lost. I couldn't hold a pencil properly, catch a ball, or ride a bike. Anything that required a sequence of tasks in quick succession or any sort of transition between tasks was very difficult. I would forget what I was meant to be doing before the teacher had even finished giving instructions to the class. This often meant I'd spend a lot of time wandering around the class, or simply sitting doing nothing. I would forget where my desk was if I was away from it for more than a few seconds. I would forget what peg I had used, what colour my jacket was, and where I had put my bag. In winter I would always come home without the hat that I had left with that morning or would be missing a glove. I lost and misplaced things at school regularly, but this wasn't flagged as a concern until much later. My parents believed what they had been told by the doctors, when I was younger, which was simply that I would always be slower and take longer to catch up. And they believed that this was all it was – at least until I had been in primary school for a couple of years, at which point all my difficulties became more apparent.

Anything as a child that required balance, hand–eye coordination, or fine motor skills was a challenge for me. I struggled to fasten buttons and close zippers. Even now, I deliberately choose clothes where the fastenings aren't too small to grasp, or diffi-cult to close. School sports days were interesting, to say the least! Because of my problems with coordination and balance, I've always been an awkward runner. I have never been able to bend my knees when I run and so run from my hips instead. This didn't stop me from trying to keep up in games, but it meant that I always looked like I was going to trip or fall over, though I never did!

I vaguely remember learning to skip during break time at primary school. I would constantly trip over and couldn't judge when to jump. Eventually I would pick it up, but it took me weeks of try-ing. Games like hopscotch didn't come naturally because of my poor balance and trouble coordinating my left and right sides, and I was always very slow. I didn't learn to ride a bike without stabilizers until I was ten. I couldn't keep my balance and pedal at the same time and would always fall over. I would practise on the grass behind my nannie's house, but it took me a long time to figure out how to keep my balance. I remember one memo-rable incident where I was at my other grandparents' house, and I was riding a bike without stabilizers, with my uncle holding the back. I was managing quite well – but I felt something was off and turned round to find he had let the bike go before I promptly crashed into a tree. I also had, and still have, a tendency to stim by flapping my hands when I'm stressed, excited, or have a lot of nerves or energy, and this is something that as a child was impossible to hide.

I was unable to tie my own shoelaces until I was around 10 or 11 years old and resented that I had to wear shoes with "babyish" Velcro fastenings instead. Despite my best efforts,

I struggled with the positioning of my fingers and the process of how to tie a bow. I pressed too hard when I wrote, and always had a sore hand after writing. I've since learned that writing challenges are very common in people who have dyspraxia (Kirby, 2023). Despite this, my writing was neat for my age, and I loved reading. At one point I had more than 50 books by my favourite author Lucy Daniels, the *Animal Ark* series, and I had read them all, repeatedly. I enjoyed English, and I began writing short stories for fun at the age of ten. My favourite week of the school year was always the book fair. Nevertheless, I struggled to hold a pencil or write for long periods. You can always tell when I get tired writing by hand, as my writing starts off very neatly, but becomes less and less legible as it goes along. I have always written with my paper at an angle, but as a child this annoyed one particular teacher who would always straighten my paper as she walked past, and then she'd get frustrated when my writing inevitably became messy. I would eventually tell her that if she wanted my writing to be nice, she had to let me write the way I wanted.

My fear of getting lost meant that I worried about leaving the class alone, and as a result from around six years old I completely refused to use the toilets at all at school, waiting until I got home. This was the case almost up until I left school. My anxiety around bathrooms is something that has persisted my whole life, and it is very rare that I will use public toilets unless someone I am with is going at the same time or I know exactly where I am. In primary school I remember drawing a brain (really a circle with wobbly edges). I coloured in half of it black, half of it left white, with a line down the middle and a large question mark. I can't remember whether it was part of a school project, but it must have been. I was definitely aware of my differences, even if at that point I couldn't fully grasp what it meant. As a child and definitely in my teens, I was frustrated by the fact that I struggled with simple tasks, and angry that I couldn't do many of the things my peers took for granted.

Unapproved disclosure of disability – the bullying begins!

The summer when I turned 11, we moved house, and my sister and I had to move schools. My sister is outgoing, confident, quick witted, and makes friends easily. She didn't seem fazed at all by the change, and I was always a bit jealous that she managed to slip in and instantly make friends. I was a fish out of water. Up until this point, my day-to-day life had never really changed in any significant way, and it was a huge shock. I found it next to impossible to get used to a new school, new routines, and new people, and I hated it. I struggled to make friends and spent a lot of time alone. I did eventually meet my best friend Rae a month or so later. She has dyslexia and many of our struggles were similar. But my naivety and willingness to see the best in anyone meant that I attracted children who I believed were my friends, but who really just wanted to take advantage. I was an easy target for bullies, who quickly became aware of my clumsiness, difficulties with memory, and tendency to lash out when I was cornered – which only made the bullying worse.

In the face of bullying, what I didn't realize, however, was that my disability had been disclosed to students without permission. I was certain that I had never said anything to anyone about my disability at that point, but all the children in my year seemed to know anyway. I just assumed that the other children had picked up on the fact that I have a tendency to repeat myself, that I am clumsy, and that I walk with a limp. In fact, this wasn't the case. My class had been told by the teachers that I had amnesia. Obviously, this was incorrect, but the damage was done. Had that never happened, I believe my school years would have panned out very differently. As a kid, all I ever wanted was to be "normal". I can pinpoint the day when this happened, because I had been sent out of class – bizarrely, to feed birds. I remember being handed a bag of bread and told to go outside. I would have been around ten years old when this happened, but despite my age, I was acutely aware this was out of the ordinary. I remember thinking at the time that it was a bit strange, but it would never have occurred to me to question a teacher's instruction. They had sent me out of the room to – poorly and inaccurately – explain my disability to the class. I only found out about this after speaking to my best friend years later, and my family only knew when I told them when I started writing this book. My mum was gobsmacked. It didn't occur to me to mention it at the time. I had always assumed that the school had sought permission from my parents before they did that, or at least informed them of their intention, but they never knew.

The more I thought about the unapproved disclosure of my disability, the angrier I became! Disclosure of disability should never be a decision for a teacher or school to make independently from parents and students themselves. I still fail to see the logic in the decision-making, if there was any at all. As an adult I still can't comprehend why anyone thought this was a good or sensible idea. That they could have possibly thought it was a sensible choice is mind-blowing to me. I honestly believe that this was a decision made not to make my life easier but was simply the staff's way of absolving themselves of any responsibility. After all, how could they be held responsible for how students reacted once they were told? I was bullied relentlessly from that point on, and I can never forgive the teachers responsible for putting me into that position. As you'll soon discover in the following chapter, bullying would become even more prevalent in my secondary school experiences.

3
Secondary school experiences

Commencing secondary school and a disruption to routine

In secondary school, I had a hard time adapting to the huge changes in my daily routine. My sister is ten months younger than me, but people often assume she is the oldest. When we were both at the same school, it was easy for me to go to her if I had any problems. However, the jump from primary to secondary school was terrifying! For my first year at secondary school, I didn't know anyone who really knew how to help me, and I found the transition overwhelming. While primary school was a relatively small building, on one level, and had only a handful of teachers, the secondary school had three floors, outbuildings, and a different teacher for each subject. I think it took me months to be able to find my way around confidently.

My problems with short-term memory meant that I needed the assistance of an auxiliary, both in class and finding my way between different classes. The role of auxiliary teachers is to assist students with disability (Mullai, 2019). This support, however, only served to further highlight my struggles and differentiate me from my peers. By this point I was acutely aware of my disability, and embarrassed that I didn't blend in with the crowd. I would try in vain to explain my situation to my classmates – I had a very good grasp of what my condition was by that stage, but my attempts to explain it only made the bullying worse.

I can't remember exactly when I had my first panic attack, but it happened while I was still in school. I do remember the horrible heaviness in the pit of my stomach and how I suddenly felt dizzy, and everything started spinning, seemingly out of nowhere. I think they are triggered by unpredictable situations, or if I anticipate something unexpected or unpleasant happening. Luckily, they seem to have largely disappeared over time, although I still experience intense anxiety in most social situations, even when I'm with family members or my oldest friends.

Nothing obvious has ever happened to cause my anxiety. I have always had a tendency to panic, for instance if someone is late, or there are last-minute changes to plans. I have persistently found even small changes incredibly difficult to cope with. I thrive on routine and consistency, which is somewhat ironic as I find it nigh on impossible to build or stick to any kind of schedule or routine. I have always tended to avoid or to put off anything new, simply because I find change so challenging. When I moved into secondary school, I didn't have that reassurance. Because of how far we lived from the school I had to get the bus. My difficulties with speed and depth perception meant that I could not cross the road alone as I couldn't tell how fast cars were going or how close they were to me. Additionally, I would forget to check for approaching traffic and use crossings when crossing the road, I would simply be focused on where I needed to go and start walking, oblivious to the safety protocol. I had the assistance of an auxiliary in most practical subjects, like woodwork, chemistry, and art, and needed help in computing. I always found it easier to learn by doing, but my memory problems and subsequent safety concerns made it impossible to do so alone. I struggled to listen to the teacher and write at the same time, and so the auxiliary would often write for me to allow me to concentrate on what the teacher was saying.

The bullying worsens!

I would regularly find my schoolwork and folders had been deliberately hidden so I would get confused, and my schoolbag was regularly moved around the classroom. I needed my routines, and for everything to be in the same place, and I would panic and get embarrassed and upset when I couldn't find my stuff, which my bullies found funny. I had food thrown at me in the canteen. I would find myself being tripped and shoved in the corridors and pushed on the stairs between classes. The students had a number of very enlightened nicknames for me such as spaz, spastic, thick, stupid, and the name of our local mental health unit. At break and lunchtimes I hated sitting in a crowded, noisy room, and would eat very quickly or not at all, just to escape the noise and crowds. I think that's probably where my anxiety around eating and going out started. To avoid the bullies, I would usually either go to the library on my own or sometimes simply hide in the stairwell until it was time to go back to class. I occasionally went out, but I would be met with groups of students shouting names wherever I went, and I found it really difficult not to react. It was eventually decided at some point during my second year that I would be kept inside the school at break times, to "keep me safe". This was, in fact, simply because the school found it easier to keep me inside, rather than punish my bullies.

Mathematics was my worst subject. While I could look at a page in English classes and instantly see what I needed to do, maths work was impossible to understand and was like reading another language. I had a very poor grasp of anything to do with numbers and found maths classes stressful and draining. To help, the school decided to put me into the learning support base. Even though I found maths stressful, I actually enjoyed being in a separate class. I had few friends, and it was a relief to be away from my classmates. I always remember "the base" – it was a huge room, which I seem to remember had beanbags somewhere but that might be wrong. It was given a makeover from the dreary, sad, grey beige of the rest of the school and was painted bright sunflower yellow shortly after I started first year. My best friend Rae was also in the base for maths class, so I didn't feel completely alone. I always remember the learning support teachers, particularly Mrs Gray who had short, platinum blonde hair, wore beautiful summer dresses and coral lipstick regardless of the weather, was always immaculately made up, and is one of the kindest people I have ever met.

Because of my significant difficulty with maths, I remained in the learning support base until I was going into my last year, when for some reason they made the decision to move me into the main maths class. This still puzzles me because while the maths teacher was very nice and tried her best to help me, I was constantly falling behind and needing extra help, and I didn't understand why they didn't leave me in the base. All moving me into the mainstream class achieved was to ramp up my anxiety and make me afraid to answer questions for fear of being singled out. I would often wonder why it had to have been me that was born like this.

High school and physical education – a new kind of nightmare!

Dyspraxia causes muscle weakness, and poor balance and fatigue are commonly associated with the condition (Dyspraxia Foundation, 2024). According to the Dyspraxia Foundation (2024), children with dyspraxia experience "struggles in physical education (PE), especially during team games when the environment is constantly changing. Movements appear awkward and effortful." So PE was a special kind of nightmare. I was never chosen when the class was split for team sports, and the team that had the misfortune of having me on their team made it clear that I wasn't welcome. I couldn't really hold a bat properly. I struggled to catch, hit, throw, or kick a ball (I still do). The other kids were acutely aware of this. This usually meant I'd have a ball thrown at me as hard as possible as I wasn't fast enough to get my arms in front of my face, or I'd be tripped or pushed as I was taking part in games. I was clumsy and slow and would forget what team I was part of. I just couldn't understand games like rounders, football, and basketball, as I find recalling a series of instructions next to impossible.

I desperately wanted to be accepted and briefly joined the girls after school netball class in my first year of secondary school, but realized very quickly that I wasn't welcome. After what felt like years (but was probably weeks) of constant name calling and nasty comments, coupled with how much of a challenge I found it physically, I quit. My PE teachers were fortunately sympathetic, as they could see how much I struggled with the subject, thanks to my coordination, poor spatial awareness, and the continuous bullying from the other kids. But there was only so much they could help with. After two years of this, I was eventually excused from PE permanently and would go to the learning support base to catch up on work or read while my classmates were in the gym. My bullies never faced any consequences for their actions, beyond occasional half-hearted warnings from teachers that weren't acted upon.

In secondary school, I started napping in the afternoon when I came home. This wasn't a conscious choice, but rather because I was exhausted from physical activity and couldn't push myself any further. I was desperate to fit in and keep up with the rest of my year but was increasingly finding that it just wasn't possible. Even now, I still nap in the afternoon, otherwise I will get a headache and can't concentrate. If I try to push through despite my fatigue, I feel lightheaded and sick, and I have been sick on the occasions that I can't stop and rest before carrying on with my day.

My high school bullying experiences from a reflective standpoint – lessons to be learned!

As an adult, looking back at the bullying I endured in high school makes me really angry! The bullying was a daily constant, even taking place in or between classes, and most teachers just acted as if it weren't happening. I was always told to "just ignore it". The traditional school of thought seems to be that childhood bullying is something that just happens, an inevitability for those of us who have the misfortune of not fitting the invisible moulds that society tells us we should. But while I understand that preventing bullying entirely isn't possible, more should be done to support and protect those who are more vulnerable to bullying, without making them feel like they are the problem. I have neurodivergent friends who have their own horror stories of how they were treated at school, and unsurprisingly they are very similar to my own. The adage "sticks and stones may break my bones, but names will never hurt me" is a lie. Words last far longer than any physical injury, stick in your head for far longer than they should, and destroy your confidence and self-esteem in the process. I remember all the insults that were levelled at me, and the words "thicko" and "spaz" still rattle around my mind when I have a bad day.

I believe the bullying that I suffered could have been lessened or avoided entirely if the school had simply asked my own and my parents' opinions. As it was, I feel like I was simply "thrown to the wolves" because of the school's poor understanding, lack of knowledge, and absence of appropriate training. It just seemed like they couldn't be bothered with making any effort to protect me. I think that the education system is still poorly equipped to understand and support neurodivergent people in general, but dyspraxia still seems to be lesser understood and accommodated than other, more well-known conditions. Children with dyspraxia continue to miss out on the school supports that they need (Dyspraxia Foundation, 2024). I hope in time that this will change. But neurodivergent people need to be listened to. We know our conditions better than anyone, have dealt with more than our fair share of obstacles, and have a better understanding of what is needed to remove barriers to a fair education. From what I have seen, read, and experienced myself, bullying simply isn't enough of a priority within the UK school system. Students' mental health and performance suffer as a result and parents are forced to make the impossible choice of disrupting their child's learning by removing them from school, or by continuing their education with a target on their backs and little or no protection from bullying.

There seems to be a prevailing attitude that those in authority know best. But unless they have a disability or are neurodivergent themselves, I don't believe they can fully comprehend the implications of their actions. I hope in the very near future and with an ever-increasing understanding of neurodivergence that this will change. The bullying of neurodivergent and disabled children is something that could be reduced by including neurodiversity and disability education in the school curriculum. Some people may make the argument that this isn't necessary, but I believe at a young age education about all disability, and removing the mystery surrounding hidden disability in particular, would go a long way in normalizing hidden conditions by fostering patience and more empathy. This could drastically reduce bullying and anxiety for children who are targeted and ostracized simply for being themselves.

I believe that the best way to address the misconceptions, stereotypes, and stigma of disability is through normalizing awareness and talking about disability issues freely, without the undertones of fear or pity. Disability is more common than people think, with one in five people in the United Kingdom being disabled (Government UK, 2022). Despite this, people with disabilities face prejudice and misunderstandings at every turn, particularly when disability cannot be seen. This is something that I find bizarre. We are now well into the twenty-first-century and information about inclusion, disability, and neurodivergence is more readily available than ever before. There is simply no excuse for leaving individuals to struggle with their conditions alone when there are so many options for help available.

Getting away from high school bullying

I made the decision to leave high school at 16. That decision was all that got me through my last year. I finally reached a point where I'd had enough of the constant bullying, and just wanted to get out! In retrospect, I wish I had chosen to change schools and completed the last two years of high school. It is my hope that neurodivergence becomes more widely understood within education, and that students who are grappling with dyspraxia will be diagnosed far earlier and not be left to deal with the consequences of a school system that often treats them as inferior.

4
College experiences

College and course accessibility challenges

During my last year of school and just before I turned 16, I applied for college. There was little reasoning behind it, I had simply had enough of being bullied and wanted to escape. I still have an old school report which states, "Kimberley has applied for several colleges, she doesn't really know what she wants to do, everything seems to be centred around 'escaping from school.'" This was indeed the case, but only because I had been failed so badly by a system that seemed to place an inherently higher value on the education of neurotypical students. Those of us with minds who work differently to the norm are routinely ignored or actively excluded simply because it requires too many resources or too much effort to accommodate our needs and give us adequate support. The availability of such support can help to build on strengths relating to neurodivergence (e.g. empathetic, attention to details, strong motivation) (Armstrong, 2012). I believe I could have completed higher education and gone a lot further than I did in my studies, but I would have needed help that the school would not have been interested in providing. The irony is, many of the most beneficial accommodations for neurodivergent individuals are inexpensive or free and require little effort to implement. The school did everything they could to push me towards college, and I don't believe it was anything to do with my education. I believe they had simply had enough of trying to support me. I would have loved to have studied higher English, but you weren't allowed to study only one subject. I enjoyed learning even though it was more challenging for me, and had things worked out differently I would have loved to have completed my last two years of school. But the bullying I had suffered for more than half of my school years meant that I couldn't even think of that option. I was simply desperate to escape! In retrospect, I wish I had followed a different route and tried to finish school, but at the time I had had enough.

The school had made the decision, on the basis that I still needed a lot of help and support, that a college course aimed at students with learning difficulties would be suitable. I was quite happy with the decision at this point because school had in the main been a miserable experience. I was just relieved to have an alternative. This course was basically a bridging gap between school and work. I attended a school link course involving spending one day at college per week, and four at school. I believe the thought behind this was that it would help me settle into college faster when I eventually started. I was looking forward to the beginning of the term. However, when my first day came, it was nothing like what I had been told nor what I expected. I was bored, learning nothing, and couldn't find anyone else who was similar to myself, as I had expected there would be. I had been placed in the wrong class, a class where the severity of the disabilities and support needs of the students were far greater than my own. Not wishing to seem rude or as though I was saying I was better than the people I was with, I remained in the class for a few weeks before I voiced my concern about having been placed in the wrong course. I was told I had been placed in a different class because the head of the course believed this class would be more suitable. My family and I decided to challenge this decision, which meant withdrawing from college until a solution was reached.

We received a very rude, condescending, and patronizing letter from the college shortly after, in which they outlined their reasons for placing me in the class they had. Their decision was ultimately centred around the fact that I couldn't travel independently. While my parents were in the middle of drafting a reply, I decided to write my own response. I couldn't understand why they had made the decision that I thought was ridiculous. I sat down and wrote a two-page letter outlining why I believed their decision was unfair and was determined to send it. But my parents decided that, while technically correct, my version was a bit too direct and blunt to have the desired effect. So they decided to tone it down a bit before sending it. However, this revision had no bearing whatsoever on their decision, and I would spend almost a year in limbo before starting college on the course that I originally applied for. This commencement followed a drawn-out dispute and was after I was able to travel independently. The fact that this was such a big issue in accessing a course supposedly designed to support disabled people still stuns me, and I think speaks volumes about how many neurodivergent people are treated throughout higher education and recruitment in general.

Whether or not I could travel independently didn't affect my ability to complete the course. I have since concluded that many of these types of "rules" are made not to assist disabled individuals, but to make life easier for those who make the decisions. There are so many unnecessary barriers for neurodivergent people in education, and it wouldn't take much to make these barriers disappear. This is a perfect example of why disabled and neurodivergent people should be consulted and included on boards, panels, and as part of company management teams. The irony is, the needs of most neurodivergent people are not particularly complex or difficult to understand. But organizations need to be open to listening to and learning from us. Sadly, the fact is that many are not interested in people with disability (Polman and Parker, 2024).

Travelling to the course on my own

While my course access problems were happening, my family learned about and contacted a local organization who taught individuals with disabilities how to travel independently. I had to learn everything about travelling on my own. At that stage I wasn't able to make sense of the bus timetables, never mind where to catch a bus. At first, I met up with a "buddy", Sam, who would come with me to catch the bus and travel with me, reminding me of things such as where to find the bus stop and to use the crossings. Travel is one of the many things that people assume I do not have any trouble with because I have no physical disabilities. But my dyspraxia means I have little sense of danger, and no sense of direction, and this is further magnified if I am in an unfamiliar place. At this point, I hadn't ever been far from home on my own. On the rare occasions that I would go out, I would be on the phone constantly to get directions and check where I was going, and I would always be dropped off and picked up by my family.

Because my dyspraxia affects my speed and depth perception, I am unable to judge the distance between myself and traffic or the speed of oncoming traffic. As a result, my family were reluctant to allow me to go out on my own. I had no "road sense" and would forget to look before crossing the road and to use crossings. I would be so focused on getting to where I needed to go that I would just cross the road at any particular point without stopping to check if it was suitable or safe first. I think it's safe to say that my family were more anxious about me travelling to college than I was.

My severe short-term memory problems affect how quickly I learn. I learn by repetition, and it can take weeks or months before an action becomes automatic. I worked with Sam and the independent travel company for at least a few months. Firstly, she would travel with me on the bus, and take me into town, so I could orientate myself and learn where to catch the bus, use crossings, and travel without getting anxious. I wrote everything down and followed it to the letter. While I learn in much the same way as other people, more often than not I need to break down instructions to understand them, as there are usually multiple instructions included in one step. I learn at a slower pace than most people, and it takes me longer to memorize new tasks.

I repeated the same route and routine daily for around six months. I would meet Sam at the bus stop, and we would take the bus into town. Even simple things such as the bus being a few minutes late or using a different route would make me panic, so to speed up the process and make sure I didn't get over-whelmed, we used the same route and stops each time. Because I have trouble differentiating between my left and right, and at that point wasn't familiar enough with street names to know where I was, we used shops and landmarks as markers instead. I still do this today when learning new routes. Once I became familiar enough with the route, and remembered to always use the crossings, Sam would follow my lead. This happened gradu-ally, until one day Sam told me that she wasn't coming with me. By that point I was more comfortable(ish) about travelling alone. I went through the whole thing the way I had been shown, until Sam materialized at the end and told me that she had been fol-lowing me the whole time. I could now travel safely to college on my own.

Commencing college – the good and the bad

Upon commencing college, I really enjoyed it, though the course was (and still is, some 20 years later) heavily geared towards pushing those with additional needs into hospitality and retail roles. In the first year, you were able to try all the different classes before narrowing down your choices in your second year. For that first year we had classes in cookery, retail, and administrative and computer skills. I found the cookery classes impossible. They took place in large, commercial kitchens, and while we had a high degree of support, it only served to highlight my difficulties in the kitchen. I remember little about it. But I do remember we cooked every couple of days and were encouraged to eat our own cooking, which as someone who wasn't confident in the kitchen, I was reluctant to do. I also remember that rather than using oven mitts, we used tea towels to remove dishes from the oven as these allowed for better grip. One day, I had finished cooking for the day and grabbed my tea towel as usual – but it was wet, and my hand stuck to the hot dish I had just pulled from the oven. Unsurprisingly, this isn't a mistake I've ever made again! Though even now I prefer using tea towels over oven mitts when I'm cooking – I always make sure they're dry first.

Retail classes were a mix of written work and role play, which I found awkward and difficult. After all, as I had never worked in a shop before, how was I supposed to know what was expected? The only thing that sticks out as even vaguely useful was my one day a week placement in the John Lewis cosmetics department. Ultimately, I always regretted not choosing the admin route instead of retail, because for many years I worked every weekend, and throughout Christmas and New Year. I didn't mind the admin classes, but I was always very slow at typing and picking up different processes, and I was painfully self-conscious about it. The only thing that stopped me choosing admin was a lack of confidence, which looking back makes me feel a bit sad. While I enjoyed my time at college, it gave me little in the way of qualifications or practical skills I could use. I still had no idea how to look for a job, write a curriculum vitae (CV), or what employers looked for in interviews. I would eventually dabble in higher education down the line. I took an English higher evening class in my late 20s which I would ultimately fail. A couple of years later, I briefly tried a one day a week university access course which I would also fail. But, like my time in school previously, there was no adequate support. The university had promised an auxiliary and a scribe, but this never materialized. I struggled for around three months and had to give up. Similar to my time in school, I found it difficult to listen and write at the same time and still be able to absorb what was being said.

A need for college education to be more inclusive of neurodivergent students

Ultimately, I think that there had been too big a gap between my school years and trying to return to education. But I was still shocked at the lack of support, particularly when I had made it clear I would find it impossible to continue otherwise. Typically, it is not a lack of skill or intelligence that holds back neurodivergent individuals, but a lack of empathy and appropriate support and accommodations. Neurodivergent people deserve better! We are capable of far more than we are given credit for, and often typically shunted into education and employment where we will require the least amount of support, regardless of our abilities, aptitudes, or skills. It is my hope that dyspraxia becomes more commonly known, understood, and ultimately supported, allowing us to fulfil our educational goals.

5
Employment experiences

Experiences with a Disability Employment Service

After finishing college shortly before I turned 18 and applying for jobs with no success, I found myself at the Job Centre. I will never forget them saying, "I don't know why you're here, there is no way you are ready to find a job." I didn't know where to start to even look for work, never mind how to fill out an application form, write a CV, or complete an interview.

The Job Centre then made the decision that led to me being referred to a local Brain Injury Employment Service. It felt strange at first because everyone was quite a bit older than me, but I quickly settled in. I've always got on better with people who are younger or older than me rather than the same age, and I understand this is very common among neurodivergent people. I do wonder, though, if it is a true neurodivergent trait or simply because, as children and adolescents, we are commonly bullied or isolated by our peers, and so naturally gravitate away from them. I was the youngest person in the service by around five or six years. The gentleman who started at the same time as me was in his mid-60s at the time, and we got on well. Most of the people there had acquired brain injuries, either from accidents, strokes or brain bleeds, or tumours. I was the only person with a lifelong disability. I did think at the time that that made me lucky because, as much as my dyspraxia really affects my life, I've never known anything different. I don't know what it's like to be neurotypical. I think it would've been far worse to be an independent and self-reliant adult, to suddenly find your life drastically altered.

I met an ex-police sergeant who had developed "acquired dyspraxia" in his 50s and was forced to retire after developing a brain tumour. Another woman was an ex-nurse who was no longer able to practice after her brain injury caused her to go blind in one eye. I would spend nearly five months at the Brain Injury Employment Service, starting in the morning, but always finishing at 2 p.m. While I was there, we learned practical skills for job hunting like CV writing and filling out applications, as well as classes to help us understand our brain injuries better. But one of the best things that they did to help me was to give me a diary. I have always had dozens of notes written in multiple notebooks, on random bits of paper, and in my mobile phone notes app. But this was the first time I had ever tried using a diary, and the impact on my day-to-day life was immediate. My very poor memory eats up a lot of my energy, simply because of the extra effort required to learn and remember things. But with everything in one place, it became simpler to keep everything organized. I carried it everywhere and wrote down absolutely everything I needed to remember or do on a given day.

Employment and Disability Assessments

Some people simply won't accept that I am disabled because they don't expect someone who has a severe disability to be articulate, intelligent, to have reasoning, or to be able to think for themselves. Those with unseen disabilities are often seen as pariahs by society, worthless leeches, who scam hard-working people for benefits and other supposed perks. This is largely reinforced by wider society, particularly the media, which publish sensationalist and ableist stories that are baseless both in fact and compassion. Being articulate is seen as a red flag, because based on these outdated and unfair stereotypes, you are not supposed to be able to look or sound even remotely normal, much less intelligent. To look this way is to be doubted, penalized, and forced to endure medical assessments with individuals who are frequently not doctors, much less specialists in your specific disability. Any sniff of intelligence is misconstrued and seen an attempt to fake a disability, and frequently leads to more intrusive, intense, and stressful scrutiny.

Many disability assessments are carried out over the phone, frequently by people with little or no knowledge of your particular disability. Questions are deliberately vague and often leading. Compassion is scant and there is often a tendency towards a suspicious or aggressive attitude. For me, this creates a huge amount of stress and worry. My family often have to step in to help me, as I get incredibly upset and uncomfortable as I feel like I am being targeted because I'm built differently.

While I appreciate that it's impossible to have an in-depth under-standing of every disability, it is grossly unfair that people with disabilities are forced to educate, explain, and defend themselves to others who have no base experience or understanding of their condition to begin with. I had an assessment recently, where I had to try to explain my disability in a half-hour phone call to someone who had never heard of dyspraxia. It is really frustrating because, while it isn't very well publicized compared to many other conditions, dyspraxia isn't rare. It wouldn't be difficult to find a knowledgeable person and make the whole process far less stressful.

I remember once having a disability assessment, where the doc-tor I spoke to asked to look at my diary, and he opened it and laughed. He is the only disability assessor I have had to date who knew anything at all about dyspraxia; as it turned out, his nephew was dyspraxic. He told me exactly what my difficulties were, and why. He said that when he opened my diary, he saw exactly what he expected – excessive detail and long-winded explanations. But that's the only way I can remember what I'm doing, one-or-two word reminders don't work for me because my memory can't be "jogged" in the same way as a neurotypical person. My attempts at organization are chaotic at best, and my diaries (when I don't lose them) are a mismatch of quick barely legible scribbles and weirdly specific details. The calendar and notes apps in my phone have hundreds of notes and screen-shots, which would make little sense to anyone but me. But if I'm not specific enough I won't remember what it was that I needed to remember by the time I came back to it. I have had periodic and very stressful disability assessments every few years, but he said that as long as he had something to do with it, I wouldn't have to worry about them again. I have met the odd doctor or disability assessor who has been understanding or willing to listen. But most aren't knowledgeable, and it makes the whole experience worse. I have had to attend multiple medical assessments and benefit appeals over the years, where my knowledge frequently outstrips that of those who approve or deny the application, which blows my mind. I have been assessed by doctors in the past who have never heard of dyspraxia, never mind having a working knowledge of how it affects people.

The only physically obvious hints of my disability that are always present are an eye squint and a limp on my left side. Otherwise, there's nothing visible to hint at my disability at all. I walk looking at my feet, and I don't move my arms when I walk. My mum and sister were greatly amused by this. Once many years ago, we were discussing how I walk differently to other people, and it came up that I don't move my arms when I walk, they just stay at my sides. They were adamant that surely that wasn't the case, of course I moved my arms! I can't, because it throws me off balance. I started walking around the living room with my mum and sister watching me, in stitches laughing. "Move your arms!" I tried, but couldn't move my arms at the same moment as my legs. I would start walking and swing my arms, then lose my balance, wobble and fall over. The second I didn't consciously think about it, my arms stopped moving. I think it's likely because my balance is so bad, I think I must have subconsciously tried to compensate for it.

I'm unsure whether the lack of awareness surrounding dyspraxia and other invisible disability in the workplace lies in a general ignorance of it, or whether negative portrayals of disability perpetuated by mainstream media are to blame. Neurodivergent people are portrayed by the media at extremes, as slow and not particularly bright, usually with obvious physical tics – or extraordinarily intelligent people who are charming and just the acceptable amount of awkward or quirky, blunt, and rude with zero social skills. Negative reporting on neurodivergence in the mass media can promote stigma (Mellifont, 2019). The character Sheldon in *The Big Bang Theory* is a great example of this – though never told he has any formal diagnosis, it is often subtly hinted that he is neurodivergent in some way. The reality is that most of us land somewhere in the middle, where we have enough social skills to blend in, but we find it challenging and tiring. My energy levels and often anxiety makes it challenging to maintain multiple close friendships as I find socializing tiring, and so don't want to go out as often. We are considered bright, but often "for someone like you". Or just told that we can't possibly be disabled because we are often adept at observing and copying other people's actions and masking our difficulties to fit in. Masking involves the hiding of neurodivergent traits in efforts to seem to be neurotypical (The Brain Charity, 2023).

Commencing employment

I eventually got a seasonal job working in a huge clothing stockroom, and I always remember the interview. It was the first interview I had ever had, and I didn't have a clue what to do, or what to expect. I had tried to memorize facts about the company, and unsurprisingly that was a mistake. I was very worried and so nervous that I had a meltdown in the interview, swore after forgetting my answer mid-sentence, before panicking and stopping talking completely. I came out thinking I'd get nowhere. But much to my shock, the next day I got a phone call from him saying that he wanted to offer me a job. I spent three months working in their stockrooms, sorting, tagging, and hanging stock to go out on the shop floor. When I applied, I had expected to be on the shop floor, but I really enjoyed it. It was a seasonal job, and so I was only there for three months. But I now had some work experience to help me going forward.

I would briefly have another seasonal job a couple of months later. Telling them of my disability in the interview, I mentioned that it might take me longer to pick up on the till-training. They seemed understanding and said that they would do that "once I had settled in". It never happened. I spent almost two months bored out of my mind, emptying bins, cleaning, tidying up, and manning the changing rooms. There never seemed to be a manager around, and I eventually quit after realizing they had no intention of giving me any more training.

There is a prevailing "we know best" attitude towards neurodivergence in many organizations and this needs to change. The experts on neurodivergence are the individuals who live with these conditions everyday. For things to change, organizations need to be willing to open up the conversation and perhaps admit they have been wrong in the past. Too many people think that there is nothing to gain from our insights, or that any cost or effort that is necessary to level the playing field will outweigh any benefit. This is backwards thinking. Too many neurodivergent people find themselves struggling to find employment, not because they lack skills or knowledge, but because the recruitment and employment processes is skewed toward favouring neurotypical responses and behaviours such as open body language, tone of voice, and consistent eye contact, which are challenging and painful for many neurodivergent people. Employers are missing out on a huge pool of talent by refusing to consider neurodivergent candidates, just because they are unable to adhere to unspoken social norms.

Experiences as a volunteer

After going back to the Job Centre and struggling to find anything suitable, volunteering was suggested, and I found myself volunteering in a charity bookshop. My first meeting with the deputy manager Helen, was nerve-racking but we clicked almost immediately. I'd spend my shifts sorting donations, pricing books, organizing the basement stockroom, and anything else that needed to be done. I loved it. After I explained my memory problems, the manager Jen showed me how to use the till and stuck a printed list of instructions to it. So I finally had the till training that my earlier employer had refused to give me.

I watched Jen and Helen like a hawk and copied what they did and how they spoke to the customers. It worked, and I quickly became more confident. Now, I can talk to just about anyone, but it is learned behaviour – this comes at least partly from my time in retail. During my time at the bookshop, I became more confident about talking to people. Before that, speaking to anyone new terrified me and I would avoid it at all costs. I remember the first day I met Helen, and she shared a funny antidote about a doctor's appointment that she had. It was impossible not to laugh, and we bonded very quickly. During my time at the bookshop, I would learn how to do everything, including pricing rare and antique books online. We were sometimes handed antique books that people clearly didn't know the worth of. I remember one such book, which didn't look like anything special, eventually sold online for a couple of hundred pounds. A couple of years ago I found an envelope in a drawer. It contained a book that I had bought from the bookshop because I found it interesting. It was a 1960s kids' book. Money wise it wasn't worth anything, but I find old books fascinating. We always had a large number of vinyls donated, which took up most of the back wall. Inexplicably, we also received a donation of a wind-up, fully functioning 1950s record player, which we didn't sell, instead using it to play vinyl records in the shop.

I stayed for three years before the charity shut the shop down, and I cried for weeks. I would volunteer for a few different charities in the next couple of years, but I never found the same happiness in volunteering again. I volunteered in an office in the Maritime Museum, where I spent a few weeks typing out transcripts of interviews that the curator had taken. I didn't mind and found it very interesting, as I've always liked history. I would, however, have to close my eyes and sprint down the short corridor to the office, because there was a 1930s, very creepy scuba suit on display which I found terrifying. But eventually they didn't have enough for me to do, so they suggested I might be better elsewhere. I then found myself in a second charity shop purely by accident. My friend was interested in volunteering, and I tagged along when she went to talk to them. She tried it for a week and then quit. Feeling guilty about it, I stayed for around a month, but was shocked at how nasty the manager was to customers and how she spoke to her volunteers.

I then volunteered in a charity office on a Friday morning for a few months at the local children's hospital, organizing and sorting their charity tin donations for banking, when I found myself volunteering to do their fundraising 10,000 foot skydive. That was great fun. It still ranks as one of the best experiences of my life. My family were horrified but my logic was simple – I might not be able to drive, but even I can fall out of a plane. I loved it, and I have always wanted to do another one. I have always remembered more random details rather than anything useful, and this is no exception. I remember waiting to go out the door, and while the instructor was still sitting on the edge of the plane, I was left dangling out the side of the plane in mid-air. But I wasn't scared. In the plane during the ascent, I was sat between the instructor's legs facing away from him as we were clipped together, so obviously he couldn't see my face. I hadn't been nervous at all leading up to it. It had been postponed four times because of weather and timing issues, and I was excited to finally be doing it. I remember hazy bits and pieces from the day, I was quiet on the way up as I was experiencing some fear, however my excitement overtook this. What the instructor said as the plane climbed is crystal clear: "Keep talking to me." I asked him, "Why?" "So, I know you haven't passed out", he quickly replied. Apparently, it was a common occurrence. I vaguely remember the skydive, and I think that's partly why it's always stuck in my mind.

Retail work experiences

I found through my experiences that retail work can at times feel more challenging than skydiving. I felt like I had to consciously make sure I blended in and I had a system firmly in place. Remember to look at people. Remember to smile. Offer them a bag. Offer to help with packing. Ask about the credit card. Remember the special offers. Talk to them. Not too much. Not too fast. Get the shopping through quick! Have I met them before? Try to remember something we talked about (that was usually difficult, but normally they would talk about their day, and I'd find something). I almost always had notes of some description in my pocket, mostly of special offers, or something new that I needed to remember.

With most people, looking them straight in the eye for the entire conversation makes me feel oddly uncomfortable. To get around this, I simply looked at customers' eyebrows or foreheads instead, and no one ever noticed. I always felt like I was acting, and it was exhausting. I always tried to be upbeat and chatty. I couldn't switch off. I tried to be mindful of my facial expressions because I can tend to look grumpy when I'm simply tired. If I had a particularly difficult week, I'd always wear more make-up, because it felt like it let me hide. My mind was constantly working overtime. Because we only had a few minutes to each customer, I had a lot to remember to do in a very short timeframe, and it probably made me appear more erratic. My memory is maddening in this sense because a lot of the time I have to speak quickly to avoid the thought in my head slipping away. It only takes a few seconds. I can often feel when this happens and the frustration it creates is overwhelming.

I would always volunteer if the managers wanted cleaning or tidying done, as it gave me an excuse to get off the shop floor; it gave me a break from constantly having to interact with people. Strangely, I find cleaning other people's spaces simple, just not my own. It got to the point where the managers would seek me out when they wanted these things done quickly, often as there was an outside visitor or inspection due. I remember one shift when I was approached by a manager who had got wind of an unexpected visit and asked me if I would be willing to clean a room for her. I spent three and a half hours cleaning out the room off the shop floor, and it was immaculate by the time I finished. I often cleaned the tills on a Thursday night, until I was told to stop.

I never attended a work Christmas party or event as it made me too anxious to even think about it. Colleagues had been told by customers that I looked like I loved my job. But in reality I hated it most of the time. I just got progressively better at hiding it. It never felt natural. It was bearable for a few years but after a couple of rapid changes in management the atmosphere and culture got worse and worse. Unlike the charity shop, many customers were rude and entitled with ridiculous expectations. We were just told to get on with it, and customers were always backed and placated by management, however unreasonable their behaviour. After a couple of years, I learned to try and ignore it, focusing on just getting items through the till. Nevertheless, I still liked talking to some of the regular customers. By that stage I had people who would wait for me on the tills rather than my colleagues because they wanted to chat. I was told that my scan rates were considerably faster than my colleagues, and averaged around four times higher, sometimes more. But rather than being happy that I was quick and productive, I was then watched without my knowledge as they suspected I was deliberately skipping items because of my speed. I wasn't, of course. I was simply faster than most of my colleagues as working slowly was frustrating and didn't make sense to me. They didn't tell me until later that they had watched me for over a week before they were satisfied that I wasn't doing anything wrong.

We were frequently told to go faster, and so this was frustrating. I didn't understand why they suddenly decided time was an issue. I had one manager who told me, "I'm not interested if they want to talk – get them in and get them out." But that wasn't my style. I talked to the customers, but I didn't slow down because of it. I got a lot of elderly customers through my till, and they liked that I was happy to have a conversation. I was frustrated that I had done exactly as I had asked and was still penalized for it. I was also irritated by the constant background noise of the shop as I can't tune it out; I believe this is due to my premature birth. The constant overload of sounds was exhausting. I hear noises both individually and together all at once. This meant that I heard everything: the people talking in front of me, the people behind me, the tills, the card machines, the overhead fans, the doors opening and closing, and banging from the bakery. I found a local company and had custom earbuds made that still allowed me to hear but muffled surrounding noise so I could focus more easily on what was in front of me. I had always ended each shift with a headache, but the earbuds gave me some relief and meant this no longer happened. These had to be replaced a few years later after I lost the original pair.

Experiences in a toxic work environment

By the time I had been around five years in the company, something changed. Though I had many nice colleagues and got on with most people, there were a few who were allowed to bully others unchecked, and they took advantage of their positions. I became an easy target for one of these bullies, who would pick apart everything I did. They would also make snide and sarcastic comments when they were sure that no one was within earshot. After weeks of this, I raised it with management, who assured me that something would be done. However, it never was. I had dealt with bullying for long enough, and I was determined it wouldn't happen again! I would later find out I wasn't the only person she had targeted, but nothing was done about it. She would eventually leave a couple of years later after an unrelated incident, having faced no consequences for her actions. It was around this time that I developed migrainous vertigo, which made me dizzy and affected my vision, and at one point this resulted in me being signed off work for almost two months, as I couldn't stand up without the room spinning.

Shortly after my physical decline, I began looking for work elsewhere. While I had a couple of interviews, they never led to anything. It was no longer the welcoming accepting company I had joined and I was deeply unhappy. Because I worked part-time, this meant for the better part of ten years I worked every late night, Saturday and Sunday, until I started asking for alternate weekends off. I eventually received these after pointing out that I was the only member of staff who didn't have this flexibility in place. Management eventually ran out of excuses, and although my line manager wasn't happy about it, this thankfully became the arrangement up until I left. I had a few more interviews but again got nowhere. I applied for some other jobs as I saw them, but it's difficult as most positions specified full-time working, which I'm simply unable to do. After around the three-hour point, my memory and concentration begin to suffer, and I slow down.

The fact that I "only" worked part-time was a bugbear for a few of my colleagues, who would make comments about me going home "in the middle of the day". I can only work three to four hours at a time before I need to rest, or I feel physically ill. The irony was I hated being bored at work, so I often had a more productive day than many of my colleagues anyway. I had an understanding manager initially and didn't mind my job, so it didn't bother me too much to begin with. I hated being late, and was usually ten minutes early into the building, to the point it became a running joke. But because I can't judge time, I would set a timer when having my coffee at the Starbucks across the road, so I left enough time to get there. I was rarely late. I hate being late if I can help it, but because I can't judge time it can be a challenge. I couldn't use the staff canteen as it made me anxious, and I think I sat in the canteen 3 times in 13 years.

I remember a memorable shift where I was told that we had to be in for training all day as they had installed new tills, and they refused to adjust the training times for me, simply saying this was the only option. I worked from 9 a.m. until 5 p.m. before returning home and having a cup of tea, then being sick and falling asleep. I was exhausted. I slept solidly from around 7 p.m. until the next morning. When I woke up, I had a pounding headache that wouldn't clear, just from sheer exhaustion. My body felt heavy, and I didn't want to eat, it almost felt like getting a cold. I was unable to do anything but nap and watch television, and it took almost three days before I started feeling better.

At the start of 2019, the atmosphere at work had become more toxic and my head started twitching and shaking randomly. I didn't pay too much attention to it to start with as it didn't happen often, but it became more and more frequent and noticeable as time went on. By the summer it was happening daily and had become very obvious, and I would be sitting at work trying not to let people see me shaking. It was the strangest sensation, I could feel an odd, almost fizzing, rippling sensation travelling up from the middle of my back to my head before it started and I quickly realized that the more I tried to suppress it, the worse it became.

I was referred to a neurologist, who quickly diagnosed an essential tremor. But, fortunately, unlike some other conditions where the tremor is only a symptom, the tremor in my case is the condition. It is lifelong. I was told that although stress doesn't cause the tremor, it does trigger it, and makes it more noticeable. I was also told that while medication could help the symptoms and calm the tremor, they didn't always work, and in any case had a range of very unpleasant side-effects that meant the neurologist was reluctant to prescribe medication and wouldn't consider it until he had no choice. At one stage the tremor was constant, and I could feel my head twitching when I was relaxed or even trying to sleep.

As the months passed, I began to dread going to work, and started to get random migraines, stomach pains, and nausea. My essential tremor increased on the days I worked and would noticeably ramp up the closer I got to the building. My head would noticeably flicker from side to side and up and down. I would be sitting at the till serving customers and feel my head shaking, and as time went on I would notice my shoulders shaking too. The tremors got worse and worse as time went on, and a few people were starting to notice.

Being forced out!

In January 2020, two months before the UK was pushed into lockdown because of coronavirus, I was called into a meeting with my line manager. I didn't know why. I was told it was a meeting to discuss my absences from work. I was rarely off work unless I was very ill, and in this case, I had been absent with a kidney infection, and the time prior to that had been a chest infection. I always felt guilty when I had to call in sick, and often went into work when I probably should have stayed at home. I went into work when I was ill as it was simply easier, when I had friends telling me that I should be staying at home and not going to work. Calling in sick often meant you would be made to feel guilty as they were often short staffed as they didn't employ enough staff, and a lot of the time I just didn't have the energy to fight. It was easier to just go to work. You were made to feel like a criminal for being absent from work, regardless of how fit you were or not on that day. When I went back, the return to work meetings routinely felt more like an interrogation than an expression of concern and how fit you were to return at that point.

Like any other workplace, you had to meet with your line manager after returning to work after absence, but these meetings would frequently take place days or even weeks after you had been ill. After explaining my absences in a return-to-work meeting, I was told that the situation was being escalated, and I was called into another meeting a week later. I was devastated and called my mum as I was inconsolable. I had never had any incident like this before as my attendance and timekeeping had always been a source of pride. In 13 years, I had been late for work only a handful of times, and only took sick days when absolutely necessary. This meeting took place weeks after my last absence, and I always had to keep notes or look back at messages to friends to remember why I had been absent. They never called me in after the absences had happened, nor advised me I had hit any triggers. I told them I could easily get doctor's notes to verify that I had had a chest infection and a kidney infection – and I had got antibiotics and been genuinely ill when I had been off – but I was never asked for them.

After receiving a formal letter from my line manager during my shift and subsequently being called into a meeting with my manager along with a colleague to act as a witness, my manager rejected my subsequent letter appealing the decision. I was then called into a meeting with my manager and a colleague representative. I was told that I would be getting a formal written warning for absence and I was blindsided. I couldn't believe what I was hearing! I asked my manager if she was aware that employers are legally required to have a higher trigger threshold for disabled employees – this is because many of us work part-time instead of full days, and so any occurrences of absence will take more hours from your week. I will never forget my shock when my manager uttered the words, "I never knew you were disabled, Kimberley." I was speechless. And rendering me speechless is almost unheard of. It was well known within the department that if you needed me to remember anything new or different that it had to be written down, and my manager, despite the protests to the contrary, was well aware of this fact.

My colleague almost laughed; I think purely through disbelief. My line manager had at that stage been supervising me for well over two years and had been my colleague for around ten years before that. At work, I was always very open about my dyspraxia; I had nothing to hide or be ashamed of. I often chatted about it casually to customers as many of them were curious as to why I worked part-time, and assumed I was a student. I always corrected them. It is simply inconceivable that my manager was in the dark over my disability. They had known from the beginning that I had a disability, as when I was first employed it was classed as "supported permitted work" through the brain injury service I had attended. I've always worked part-time, within the allocated hours. The company were aware of this, as they would change my shift days during busy periods but take me out of another day because they knew I couldn't go over the 16-hour threshold for permitted work.

I asked for a copy of my staff records repeatedly, and after ignoring my request for weeks, I finally received a digital copy of the file. But the equal opportunities page – which in the UK asks, amongst other questions, if you are considered disabled – was missing. I didn't ask a second time; I was growing increasingly distressed by how I was being treated, and I felt like I was now being viewed as a problem to be solved, rather than the person that my colleagues had known and trusted for the past 13 years. I began to dread going into work, because I never knew what new stresses the day would bring.

At that point I started looking for another job, but it was really difficult. I had no intention of going back to retail, but I had limited experience of anything else. I carried on searching, applying for jobs that stated they needed no previous experience, but despite applying for multiple jobs over the course of the year, I heard nothing back. Most of the jobs I saw required remote working which at that point I wasn't confident I could do. But I carried on looking.

The cowardly mobbing

Mobbing involves employees working together against a target (Suskind, 2020). In this regard, I noticed subtle differences almost immediately after the meeting with my manager. A couple of managers who had known me for years and had always treated me equally started acting oddly, speaking to me slowly and checking if I understood them, which of course I did. I started to become extremely anxious whenever there was a manager around and always felt like I was doing something wrong, even though I wasn't. I carried on with my job as normal, although I was more cautious of doing anything that attracted attention or meant I needed to interact with my manager more than absolutely necessary. Even though I knew deep down that I hadn't done anything wrong, I felt like I was at fault simply for being disabled. My sleep gradually worsened, dwindling until it was almost non-existent by the time I left the company in October 2020.

I asked for a second meeting to find out why they hadn't taken the fact I was disabled into consideration. I also informed them I would be taking a family member, my sister, as I no longer trusted that my colleagues wouldn't be compromised by attending meetings with me. During this meeting, they expressed concern that my sister would be speaking for me, while all the time addressing her, instead of me, until they were pointedly told that she would never dream of speaking for me and I was able to speak for myself. Despite the fact that I had known these colleagues for years, I was treated like a stranger and spoken to as if I was slow, stupid, and unable to understand. I was gobsmacked – just when I thought nothing else could happen, it did! I pointed out that they had a sign in the corridor, with a picture of the sunflower lanyard saying "not every disability is visible", which, given the circumstances, I found ironic. They clearly weren't practising what they preached. I have noticed that many companies are guilty of this. It sounds and looks good to be disability inclusive, but to many companies that is where it ends. When I pointed out that I had one of these myself, they looked pleased, which I didn't understand – they then told me I could wear my lanyard at work. It was incredulous that they would even suggest it. I could do anything that my colleagues could do, and while I did need to take notes and be reminded often of certain things, I didn't require regular day-to-day assistance with my job by any means. For those who are unfamiliar with the sunflower lanyard, it is worn by those who have invisible disabilities when they are in situations where they may need assistance. I have worn mine in airports, at unfamiliar bus stations, and on trains, but I don't believe in wearing it all the time, only when I genuinely need help. It felt like they were now deliberately trying to highlight that they were employing someone with a hidden disability, and they wanted praise or recognition for it. I declined to do so.

During lockdowns, like other people I found many things to be difficult, but being away from work was a welcome relief. My migraines settled down. My essential tremor, which had been steadily getting worse for the past year, started to calm down rapidly to the point it had been when I first noticed it. I bought a 6.8 kg weighted blanket and started sleeping a little better. My sleep has never been great, largely because of my tendency to overanalyse my sleep and overthink my day. My mind starts working overtime as soon as my head hits the pillow. While this dispute carried on, I was lucky to sleep two and a half hours a night. But the weighted blanket provided more weight and feed-back to my muscles, which helped me relax, even if I didn't sleep. Now I won't sleep without it. I hate being touched lightly, par-ticularly if it's without context or warning. It makes me feel odd. I love tight hugs, but it feels weird if I feel like I can still move, as if it triggers something in my brain, almost like not being able to scratch an itch.

On returning to work after furlough had ended, my migraines and essential tremor returned with a vengeance, and sleep once again became difficult. I would feel sick going into work, and that would last all day. Because of the social distancing rules in place during Covid-19, we were unable to use the usual staff entrance. I requested instructions with a diagram showing where to go.

While I received some information, it wasn't clear enough for me to follow. I was handed full-sized, highlighted floor and building plans, but I found them impossible to understand, and so resorted to rewriting the instructions myself. It was as if they had decided that if were now going to give me any assistance, they were going to do it in the most awkward and inconvenient way possible. They weren't trying to be helpful, I believe this was done solely so they could say they had provided something.

"Voluntary" redundancy – a way out!

I considered taking legal action, but by that stage I was exhausted, feeling stressed out almost constantly, and just wanted everything to be resolved. At the end of the month, all colleagues were called into a meeting, where it was announced that the company would be making redundancies, and would be looking for people to take redundancy voluntarily, so they didn't have to choose themselves. I applied, along with a handful of others. I hated the thought of not working, but I was still highly stressed, burnt out, and miserable, and it eventually got to the point where I no longer had the energy to keep challenging them. At the time the UK was still in and out of lockdown, and I wasn't confident that I wouldn't continue to be bullied and targeted a second time. In retrospect, I regret my decision not to pursue legal action, but I had been completely exhausted by the way everything had played out and I didn't want to have to justify or defend my disability any longer. I believed that you only had a finite amount of time to raise such disputes, and this timeframe had elapsed.

When I found out my application for voluntary redundancy (VR) was likely to be accepted, it felt like a weight had been lifted. I began to count the days until my redundancy was officially confirmed. I waited and waited. I heard nothing. When it was eventually confirmed, almost two months later, that my application had been approved it was a relief. Tellingly, I was one of only a few people whose applications for VR had been approved, despite being told that there would be "many" redundancies. I firmly believe that this was because my employer now saw me as a problem and wanted to get rid of me.

My last day is ingrained in my mind. When I finally finished my shift at lunchtime, I expected to feel sad, angry, maybe elated, but certainly relieved. But I wasn't. I felt completely numb. After 13 years that came as a shock. Only one person even said goodbye. I was a bit hurt, but by that stage nothing would have shocked me. But after months of gaslighting and being forced to defend myself and feel like I had to justify who I am, I simply didn't have anything left. I didn't want any trace of the company left in my life – so I immediately went home, washed all my uniforms, and found all my staff cards, name badges, and keys, and shoved them in a bag.

That night, I slept like the dead, for the first time in over a year. I headed back to the store the next morning and handed everything back. I was told that I could have left it a few days, but I didn't want to. Ultimately, they really hurt me in a way I had never dreamed they would – they had questioned and attacked the core of who I was, and after all the time I had been there I had never expected it to end like that. While this was a business relationship, I still expected to have been treated better than I was.

I was in a rush to leave – I had no desire to hang around, but I was repeatedly told to "stay five minutes". I was irritated but complied. Then a manager, who I had never seen before in my life, came rushing over. He thanked me for my service, and handed me one of the £1 bunches of flowers that sat at the till. I had to try really hard not to laugh. But I wasn't done. I looked straight at him, and said, "What's my name?" He couldn't give me an answer. I left the shop shaking, binned the cheap flowers which were half-dead anyway, and went to Starbucks for my coffee – had it not been lunchtime, it would have been something far stronger. You have people who will consistently defend a large or well-known company to the end out of some misguided sense of loyalty. But some in management have no hesitation in throwing loyal and hard-working employees under the bus to save their own skins and to cover up management errors.

Struggling to return to an unaccommodating workforce

I struggled to find work. Despite submitting multiple applications for different roles over the next few months, I only had two interviews, in one of which they made it clear that they had found their candidate and were only interviewing me out of politeness. The second interview was in the library at a local university that I had interviewed with previously, and who seemed genuinely interested. However, despite knowing my qualifications prior to interview, and not specifying what they wanted, I was told during the interview that they would have employed me and I was perfect for the role, but unfortunately I didn't have a degree. Despite this, they still interviewed me, went into great detail about shift patterns and employee benefits; I still cannot fathom why they would put me through that if they weren't certain that I was going to work there. I assumed that I had the job. I'd rather they had rejected me outright. The job advert itself had not specified that they needed degree level education, and, in any case, the skills are something that could've been learned. They asked me many questions in the interview about my disability, and I firmly believe it was this rather than any relevant skills or experience that informed their final decision. I remember they reiterated to me before I left that I was their perfect candidate, and even sent me to have a look around the building, so I was puzzled as to why they didn't offer me the job. On asking for feedback, I was told again that I was a perfect fit for the role, and yet I still missed out on the job. When I asked them why they had sent me to look around if they had already made their decision, I was told that, "We thought you'd enjoy it." I was furious!

Unfortunately, this is all too common – employers are keen to appear inclusive to further their own interests, while declining to offer genuine opportunities to neurodivergent and disabled people. It looks good to have diversity in your team. But unless you are actively seeking to employ, understand, support, and promote the more vulnerable people in your organization, it is nothing more than lip-service.

6
Independent living experiences

Cooking experiences and challenges

I find cooking difficult as I struggle to concentrate on more than one thing at once and get distracted and flit between tasks. My family were worried about me leaving the gas on and forgetting about it. My awkward grip and struggles with hand–eye coordination mean that things like chopping vegetables, and moving full pans are awkward, and take longer than they should.

I never remember what is in my fridge and check it several times a day, and unless I consciously cook and freeze meals, I can easily have weeks' worth of spoiled food in my fridge, and my cupboards are messy with many duplicated items. But I never remember any of this, and this leads to me spending far more money on food than I would like. It is literally out of sight, out of mind, and I check the cupboards repeatedly.

I tend to eat the same things all the time; while my eating habits have vastly improved over the years, there are still a couple of foods that I can't eat. I can't eat solid cheese, as it makes me gag. I can easily eat melted cheese on toast or cream cheese, as it is the texture that is the problem, not the taste. I can't eat anything that feels "lumpy" or slimy, as this has the same effect. I like figs and dates, and I remember once finding a hard cheese with dates in them, and thought I'd give it a try. I sliced off a tiny piece, less than half the size of my fingernail. As soon as it touched my lips, I heaved and vomited. Neurodivergent food preferences are often seen as fussiness, but often it is because our brains and bodies will physically reject certain tastes and textures. My sensory preferences extend to my clothes, and I can't wear anything that feels is too tight around my neck, feels rough or spiky (anything wool that looks soft and fuzzy is awful for this), or has seams that are rough or that stick out. Summer clothes are a nightmare, because they are usually made of very thin, lightweight fabric, and not being able to feel anything against my skin drives me mad. I hate hot weather, as I overheat easily and can't regulate my body temperature as well as other people. When the weather gets colder, I really feel it. But despite the weather, I almost always wear hoodies because they make me feel secure. I have a heavy leather jacket that I enjoy wearing for the same reason. I always wear it when I'm out socializing because the weight of it helps to slightly reduce my anxiety.

Despite the fact that I have lived independently for many years, cooking isn't something that has ever got to the point where it comes naturally. Cooking is a huge challenge for several reasons, including the safety aspect and the number of steps involved. Most traditional recipes have steps within steps, several instructions lumped into one that frequently mean I need to break the recipe down myself. Cooking takes many of the most challenging aspects of my disability and puts them all together, which is why I tend to avoid it as much as possible. I batch cook as much as I can. More often than not, it takes an entire day to cook only two or three meals. Or I buy the ingredients, intending to cook, and then am too tired to do it, or I can't remember what I was intending to cook in the first place. Cleaning up after I have cooked more often than not takes longer than the cooking itself, and frequently takes more than a day to finish completely. Learning to meal prep was a game changer. I will often make one meal at the beginning of the week and have it all week, or when my energy is higher or I can enlist help, I will cook and freeze meals for a couple of weeks at a time.

My kitchen incidents, though regular, have largely been minor, like cuts and small burns. I get minor burns on my fingers or hands at least every other week. I have a scar on my right wrist after catching it on the oven shelf, and I still remember the one time I turned the gas up too high on the hob, setting my sleeve on fire. I've never cooked in long sleeves since. I think the one incident that frightened me the most was when I stood on a kitchen chair to get something out of a high cupboard, before losing my balance and falling off the chair. I fell backwards, hitting my shoulders off the oven and shattering the entire door. Somehow, I was fine except for some bruising and soreness.

Housework experiences and challenges

Assisting my independent living, I started looking into what occupational therapy could help me with as an adult. I knew that older people often had help from occupational therapists, and that people did have occupational therapy as adults, but I didn't know what for. So, I contacted our local council and made some enquiries. After I had a meeting with a lovely occupational therapist called Glenda, she would come to the house once a week and show me how to do the things I needed to become independent, like cooking, ironing, and how to be organized at home. I can remember that Helen, my manager at the bookshop, was bemused by my determination and remarked I must be the only 20-year-old she knew of who would ever willingly take ironing lessons. She said she was shocked that someone my age would be concerned with learning such things. There had initially been some discussion whether to see if I needed outside help from carers once I lived on my own, and I was determined that wasn't happening. I have always worked hard for my independence. I can be stubborn and I often see help from others as a humiliation and a failure on my part. At one point, my parents decided it would be helpful to have a cleaner come in. I felt embarrassed, ashamed, and defeated – what sort of person can't clean, particularly when they only have themselves to deal with? It took a lot of getting used to having someone in my house. I don't like people moving things around or touching my stuff – I admit my version of cleaning or organizing looks disorganized to other people and makes little sense, I know that. But I had to admit that it was a good idea – Gosia achieved more in three hours than I could in a week, and it stopped everything being quite so overwhelming. In a lot of ways, it just confirmed how differently I work from other people. My version of tidy was very different from hers, and she would often walk into my house when I thought I had done an okay job keeping up that week – and sigh at the chaos. We got on really well – but I always felt guilty about my struggle to stay on top of things without help. I don't seem to see it becoming more messy – I notice when I have a clean house, and I notice when my house is in chaos. But I really struggle to see a mid-point – the point when I should be tackling it.

My house is disorganized and can be chaotic, but it's not dirty. I frequently have overflowing baskets of washing or ironing as I have a tendency to completely forget about it, I don't seem to see it – until I either run out of clothes or I'm looking for something specific, which may have sat in the basket for days, sometimes weeks. When I decide to clean, defining a starting point is the biggest hurdle. I simply never know what to do first. It's overwhelming before I even get started. I will start doing one thing, then see something else that needs to be done and move on to that instead and forget to go back to the original task. This results in lots of half-finished jobs and usually more mess than when I started. This then means I get overwhelmed and makes it impossible to continue. My least favourite task is doing the dishes, because I hate the sensation of washing up gloves touching my skin, particularly when they're wet; in addition they make it harder to grip and I tend to flood the kitchen counter. I have an array of plants in the kitchen which frequently need to be rescued or revived by my family, as I forget to water them for weeks on end, then drown them in water. I have a very hardy aloe vera plant that has lasted a number of years, though I'm still not sure how.

I don't have any regular housework routines; I have tried in the past, but I forget and get distracted. I don't notice it piling up until the house is in complete disarray. Laundry often takes days at a time to complete as it tends to build up because I often forget and leave a load in the machine – which I always feel I need to wash again because it has been sitting. I always tend to use capsules instead of bottles of detergent as I would tend to forget I had dosed the machine and put in far too much, resulting in bubbles all over my kitchen. It is a similar situation both in and outside the house, because I forget I have clothes drying outside until I look. Often, I have gone to do something else midway through hanging out the washing and will leave the basket sitting outside with the laundry still in it. It can occasionally sit out overnight if I become distracted. Recently I have started sometimes taking my washing to a launderette as they have tumble dryers, and it makes everything so much faster, particularly for items like bath towels and bedding. I tend to have multiples of everything – either because I have lost it and replaced it, or because I simply don't remember I have it. I recently downloaded an app onto my phone that is designed for neurodiverse individuals and breaks down housework tasks, and it is very helpful – when I remember to use it. Even making a list doesn't always work, because I will see something else that needs done and get distracted halfway through. Even something simple like the phone ringing will make me forget what I'm doing if I stop at all.

Body doubling is a great way for neurodivergent individuals to stay on task, which can be an impossible feat otherwise. I body double with a friend on a Sunday to do housework, often she will just need to sit with the dog and remind me what I need to do – it's far more difficult to stray off task with someone else there. For years my kitchen was incredibly disorganized, until friends volunteered to sort it for me around 18 months ago. Everything was sorted, and lots of out of date and duplicated things were binned, with the remaining items sorted into categories and placed in transparent containers, and so while my cupboards are still chaotic, I have in the main been able to keep it semi-organized and at least now I can see everything I have (and no longer face the possibility of an avalanche whenever I open a cupboard door).

Changing duvets and sheets is often a challenge due to my coordination because the fastenings are often tricky to close and because I can't tell which way up the sheets are meant to go. It frequently takes a day on and off to fully change the sheets and bedding. Luckily, I found a company last year that sells coverless duvets that are machine washable, and that was a game changer. Covers with zips instead of buttons are so much easier and don't tend to come undone by themselves. Still, it often takes more than an hour from beginning to end. Because of my need for heavy pressure/feedback to my muscles, I use a 15 tog duvet in winter plus a weighted blanket; in summer I once tried a blanket, then a 4.5 tog duvet, but found it far too light to sleep properly. I always use the weighted blanket on top of another to increase the weight. When I started learning to iron, it took all of my concentration and coordination just to avoid burning myself. I frequently spilled water when trying to fill the iron. I had trouble using the buttons, as they were on top of the handle and hard to press, and I would have to stop ironing to use them. The occupational therapist came to the house one day with a steam generator iron, which had the steam trigger underneath and a large water reservoir; even though it was heavier and more awkward to move around, it was much easier to use. I have had one ever since. They are more expensive than a traditional iron, but it speeds up my ironing considerably.

I only tend to iron as and when I need to. I am easily overwhelmed if I have a lot of clothes to organize and put away and ironing piles tend to sit for weeks. I have tried several different things to make it easier, but never anything that I have been able to implement long term. Often, I find myself the day before I need something specific or usually the day of, frantically washing and drying what I want to wear. When I had a specific work uniform, I would often be pulling what I needed from the washing machine, having forgotten about it the night before, and frantically using the hairdryer to dry my clothes before ironing them, normally only a couple of hours before my shift.

In retrospect, I should have asked the occupational therapist how to organize housework or set a cleaning routine, as this is something I have always struggled to adhere to. I frequently get "task paralysis" and distracted particularly when tasks have multiple steps. I get easily annoyed by minor household things, when everything isn't just right. I need the things in my kitchen to line up or sit in a corner. My mum bought me some tea and coffee canisters a few years ago, which I wound up replacing shortly after – because they were round, and I couldn't line them up properly. It drove me crazy and I would adjust the position of them several times a day for weeks until I finally found square containers I could line up, which made me much happier. I love furniture with lines for the same reason.

Sleeping and dietary challenges

My sleep often suffers because of my anxiety, and this only started to get a little better after I bought a weighted blanket in 2020. Over the years, I have tried everything to help me sleep, including less caffeine, pillow sprays, drinking cherry juice before bed, and reducing light, but nothing ever seems to work long term. My mind seems to jump to life as soon as I try to sleep, and nothing has ever been successful in stopping it from happening. I rely heavily on caffeine to get me through the day and have done for many years. I have drunk tea since I was around eight months old as I refused to drink juice or water. Apparently, the health visitor had come to the house one day when I was a baby and had a hissy fit as my dad was giving me weak tea in my bottle. I have managed to roughly estimate that I drink upwards of 15 cups of tea a day. All I would drink as a toddler was tea or milk, and this hasn't really changed since, apart from my love of lattes. I might finish a bottle of water after the gym but that's probably it. I don't really tend to feel particularly hungry or thirsty, until I'm ravenous. I think this may be partly because I get distracted and forget about it. Because of this it's often until well into the day, when I feel lightheaded or sick, or check myfitnesspal, a food tracking app that I will know if I've eaten or not. That's if I have remembered to log my food that day. My memory, distractibility, and inability to adhere to routines extends to my eating habits, and I rarely eat at set times. I try to meal plan, but this often goes awry because unless I have written it down somewhere prominent, I will forget what I was planning to cook. I have a whiteboard in the kitchen that I always intended using for this purpose, but it never happened. I often forget to replace the pens so I don't use it that often.

The benefits of living with a comfort animal

I have lived in my home almost 17 years, and I have had the same night-time routine almost since the day I moved in. I settle the dog, lock the doors, turn the television off, then on again (this is so it doesn't go onto standby in the middle of the night – I can't sleep in silence) and write that the doors are locked in my phone. If I have forgotten to write in my phone that the doors are locked, I need to get up and check everything again. When I go out during the day, I frequently find myself turning back to check doors or windows. I have had a dog almost since the day I moved in, because I was too anxious to stay on my own otherwise. My grandparents, who I had lived with for the past four years, stayed overnight with me for the first week. I got my Springer Spaniel Kyra soon after. For around the first year, I had 14 separate labelled containers for the dog's food marked with the day and morning and evening. This eventually wasn't required, but in the beginning I would have forgotten to feed her or otherwise fed her too much because I couldn't remember if she had already been fed.

The desire to drive – challenges and frustrations

I can recall my Grandad once reading a newspaper article about a private clinic in Edinburgh which claimed they could significantly reduce the symptoms and improve the quality of life for people who had conditions such as dyslexia, ADHD, and dyspraxia. I was very sceptical; however, I read about the results that they had achieved and was quite excited at the prospect of a life without my dyspraxia. Particularly when, during our first visit, they said that there was a possibility on completion of the treatment that I'd be able to drive. That was all I needed to hear!

The exercises were very challenging and involved things I found difficult – things like standing on a balance board, sitting on a balance ball, tracking screens without any head movements, and throwing beanbags back and forth. There were always at least three or four different exercises to do in a session, three times a day, every day. Then I would go back to their centre almost three hours away, and they would carry out an assessment to see if my "symptoms" had improved. Initially, I was expecting the exercises to be challenging and was willing to persevere, but my progress was slow, and I didn't see any improvement or any changes, which I had expected to. The exercises highlighted my weaknesses, and I quickly became frustrated with the lack of progress. I started to hate the experience and saw no reason to carry on with it when there was no improvement in my symptoms or skills. Since I saw no difference after many months of trying with no progress, I eventually withdrew from the programme. I was disappointed but not entirely surprised. I looked them up online for more information when I was gathering details for this book. Perhaps unsurprisingly, they were closed down in 2012 after being investigated for making a string of false or unsubstantiated claims and subsequently went bankrupt. Looking back, it's ridiculous that I or my family fell for it. But I hated myself for a very long time because of my disability and at one time I would have done absolutely anything to get rid of it and make myself "normal".

Ultimately, I think the reason why the "clinic" was able to draw people in was because they targeted those people who felt like I did – people who were uncomfortable in their own skin – and played on their feelings of shame or embarrassment around their disability. The fact that they knew this and used it to line their pockets makes me angry. The only thing that had kept me going back there and persisting with the process was the promise that I would be able to drive at the end of the programme. Which was rubbish, of course, but not being able to drive is one of the things that frustrates me most about living with my dyspraxia, and the sole reason I wanted to try in the first place.

Learning to drive can be especially challenging for people with dyspraxia due to coordination and judgement challenges (Dyspraxia Foundation, 2020). The severity of my perceptual difficulties and coordination problems means that for me driving just isn't possible. I can't judge depth, wouldn't be able to coordinate my left and right side sufficiently to steer, drive whilst watching the road (as opposed to my feet), try to judge traffic speeds, and take in all the information that you need to react fast enough.

I tested my ability in a driving simulator at some point in my late teens, but it didn't go well. My parents own a company that buys and sells plant machinery and buggies, so there were always random vehicles lying around. At one point when I was around 16, they bought a gator pick-up. They have a very low maximum speed, so my parent felt it was safe enough to let me drive it to see if it was going to be feasible for me to drive a car. It only had a brake, accelerator, and gears, so I was hopeful. But I hadn't banked on just how bad my coordination would turn out to be. I didn't have the coordination to steer and use the clutch or brakes at the same time. I would watch my feet and end up swerving; one day I did manage to go into the fence, another time I landed in a ditch at the edge of the fence. If I switched my concentration to what was in front of me, I would be unable to use the pedals as I wasn't focused on them. Trying to steer with one hand so I could use gears was nearly impossible, so it would often stall. I only tried a handful of times, but that was enough for them to decide it was unsafe.

My inability to drive has always meant I feel like I stick out for all the wrong reasons. Most of my family can drive. My sister passed her driving test just a year after I was told I couldn't, and while I was happy for her that was tough to watch. To me, even now, not being able to drive still feels like the ultimate failure. I can find other ways to navigate around most of the things I find challenging but there is no alternative way to navigate through this, and it hurts. I still can't think about it too much or it makes me emotional. On the rare occasions that I travel outside of Aberdeen – usually by bus – it takes a ridiculous amount of effort, anxiety, and forward planning. It often means travelling at strange or inconvenient times and takes far longer than if I were to drive. I know a few people who choose not to drive even though they could, and I find their stance almost incomprehensible.

I understand that the reasons I can't drive are because of safety concerns, but it doesn't make acceptance any easier. It just feels like yet one more thing dyspraxia has taken away from me.

Travelling independently – wins and challenges

Despite my not being able to drive, being able to travel independently on public transport was life-changing. Until the work I did with the independent travel company, I had only been able to go into town with my sister, my Nannie, or my mum because of safety concerns and worry that I would get lost. But now I could go for a coffee or go for a wander round the shops in the town centre without having to rely on other people. I would go into town most Saturdays, simply because I could. But I never stayed in very long, because the noise and crowds were too much for me. I can't filter out background noises and being in crowds makes this worse. I'd hear the noises from the tills, people talking, rustling bags, and lights buzzing. Dealing with noises individually and together would ultimately become overwhelming. Consequently, I'm a creature of habit and tend to stick to the same places and things that I know. I have a very loose schedule most days, although the smallest thing can distract me and make me forget what I'm doing. Part of the reason that my schedule is not more rigid is because of my time perception, or lack of it, and I don't tend to walk, I almost always run. I go to the same

Starbucks every week and order the same coffee. I tend to read the same books and watch the same TV shows on repeat. I go to the cinema with a friend every Wednesday night and we go for a coffee and a walk at the same place most Sundays. Even though I have lived in the same city all my life, I still get lost on a semi-regular basis and often have to phone family members for directions when going somewhere new. I recently changed dentists, and it took me nearly 30 minutes to get somewhere that was a maximum distance of 10 minutes from the bus stop (all the while on the phone for directions).

7
Life learnings to support social and economic inclusion

Social challenges and ways forward

Because of the extreme anxiety that stems from my dyspraxia, I have always found socializing challenging, particularly if there are more than just one or two people. Even socializing with family can be difficult, and I never tend to stay at events like barbecues or birthday parties more than a couple of hours, if I have gone at all – that very much depends on how I'm feeling on the day.

I worry about embarrassing myself. I worry about shouting unintentionally – one of the symptoms of dyspraxia is being unable to control the rate, pitch, and volume of your voice. I also worry about saying the wrong thing, interrupting or offending people unintentionally, or getting the wrong end of the stick in a conversation, particularly in social situations where the environment is busy or there are a lot of people, as I can zone out and lose the thread of the conversation. If I am going somewhere unfamiliar, even if it is with people I know and people I like, I still get incredibly anxious and have often cancelled last minute, even when it is something I am looking forward to or would have enjoyed.

I don't like social events being sprung on me unexpectedly; I need to be able to gauge the amount of energy I have versus the energy that socializing takes out of me. When I have to socialize unexpectedly people can assume I'm in a bad mood, when more often than not it's a mixture of tiredness, anxiety, and sensory overload. I wear my earbuds when I go out, which help to dull background noise, but I also need to factor in how busy the place is, how harsh or low the lighting is, the complexity of the noise, and how much is going on generally. I become far more sensitive to noise when it is busy, so tend to avoid it. I do most of my Christmas shopping in October or November. This is done purposely to avoid the crowds, noise, music, and brighter lighting of shops and centres at Christmas time.

Exercising in a friendly setting

The only time I don't experience anxiety is when I am at the gym – though I do remember my first day at the gym when my instructor had to spend a significant amount of time coaxing me out of the changing room. I had burst into tears because I was so anxious and had refused to go in for my session. There were only the two of us in the room, but if I am doing something new or I'm unsure what's coming that is frequently all it takes to send me into a panic spiral. It's a small local gym, which is really helpful because I know everyone, can talk to everyone, and is the one place I can completely relax and where I have grown more comfortable being myself around other people. They remind me of which exercises I'm doing and lay out the equipment for me. I find movement that is continuous and more dynamic a challenge because of my balance, and I need to be constantly reminded what I'm doing during sets and how many reps I'm doing. I often need to nap when I come home from the gym. I can't always tell when I should take a break and can often push myself too hard because I feel I "should" be able to keep up with other people. Almost seven years later, I'm still at the same gym and don't know what I'd do without it. It is my safe space and my therapy. There is a misconception that disabled people can't or shouldn't be able to exercise. This simply isn't true and reinforces outdated and harmful stereotypes.

Taking on physical challenges – but not overdoing it!

In 2018, I completed a half marathon. I signed up for it at the beginning of the year after a few people had signed up the previous year, and immediately thought "What have I done?" But I spent the next six months building up my fitness. It took well over two hours, and I walked large parts of it. It's still one of my proudest achievements. I had booked the following week off and spent most of it napping on the couch and watching Netflix. I also completed a beast race (a tough mudder-style race) later that year as part of a team from our gym, and I found it even harder than the running. I was shocked by the sheer amount of coordination and balance required for many of the obstacles, but we went round the course as a team – I remember one of my teammates kindly picking me up and throwing me over hay bales because I struggled to climb them. We had to crawl under some obstacles, and because I can't crawl, it took me longer. We had to climb over net obstacles, and it really challenged my balance. There was also a water crossing at the end that really scared me – I'm wary of water anyway, and while I can swim, I'm not confident. But with my feet on the riverbed the water was up to my chest. I could have walked, but I swam it as it was faster. The last obstacle was a large water slide – unfortunately I ended up spinning round on my way down, coming off the slide and hitting my arm before going into the water backwards. I woke up the next day convinced I had broken my arm, but luckily it was just badly bruised. I spent the next three days at home alone and doing very little. I was exhausted! I get very overwhelmed by too much socializing and particularly after activities or occasions that last nearly whole days, I need time on my own to reset and give my mind time to rest. Fatigue is worse for neurodivergent people as we expend so much more energy just to complete our day-to-day tasks. Socializing can compound this, as it rolls sensory overwhelm, masking, and anxiety into one.

Avoiding bad business deals

One of the hardest things about being a person with a hidden disability is the lack of empathy and understanding when dealing with companies, particularly utilities and those who aren't shy to weaponize your disability against you as a business opportunity. I have found myself locked into poor deals and expensive mobile phone contracts after forgetting to ask the right questions. In my experience, even explaining what you struggle with in this situation doesn't help. You can almost see the cogs ticking away, and vulnerabilities are almost always seen as a boon for an easy sale. I have dealt with salespeople in mobile phone shops who have purposely ignored my requests for clarity or to slow down their questions, who are deliberately vague and who continue to fire questions and information at me that I don't fully understand. They will also purposely send you in circles and continue the "hard sell" approach, despite knowing full well that they haven't given me all the correct information.

Thankfully, you also have companies that take the complete opposite approach. British Gas has a programme specifically designed to help disabled and vulnerable customers where communication is simplified, and they spend more time clarifying any concerns or queries during phone calls. My experiences with Apple have always been nothing but positive, and they are always keen to make sure that you understand how the different features of their devices work. There are likely other companies that have great programmes to assist neurodivergent individuals, but they are not well publicized. There is a stark, troubling contrast between companies that identify vulnerabilities and are keen to help, and those that see disability as something to be exploited for financial gain.

Assisting and not scrutinizing neurodivergent people

The sunflower lanyard scheme is one way to reveal a hidden disability. I have had my sunflower lanyard since June 2016, when I flew from Aberdeen to Heathrow to visit family. I always need airport assistance, because of my memory, lack of sense of direction, and being unable to navigate somewhere new without panicking. My booked assistant was incredibly grumpy, which I understood because he was assisting four other people at once, including a wheelchair user. He kept looking over at me, and so I explained that while I didn't look like I needed help, I still needed assistance. He smiled at me, and it was like something clicked. He disappeared behind a desk and came out with a green lanyard covered in sunflowers. He told me that it was for people like me, and his demeanour had changed completely; he seemed almost excited to explain this new concept to me. Originally developed and piloted by the Accessibility team at Gatwick Airport and a collection of charities in 2016 (Hidden Disabilities Sunflower Scheme, 2024), the sunflower lanyard scheme is now adopted by companies all over the world. But despite initially being free at the point of use to those with hidden disabilities, the lanyard is now available at a price and is abused by some without disabilities as a perk or boast. This means that those of us who use it and have genuine disabilities are subject to the intense scrutiny and judgement that the creation of the lanyard was designed to avoid. This perhaps explains why some companies may be reluctant to publicize such initiatives. Because my disability is invisible, this fortunately means that I am not treated differently in public, as some people with physical disabilities are. This has both its up and downsides. It means that you are not exposed to the abuse that some disabled people experience in their lives. But it also means that you can struggle to receive the help you need and risk becoming a target for abuse when you genuinely need assistance.

Educating employers about neurodivergence and the need for accommodations

Trying to find employment as a person with a disability can be extremely challenging, as many of us, including myself, can only work set hours and/or work better at certain times of the day, which doesn't suit many employers. This often results in gaps in employment history, which again is frowned upon. Disabled people are often unfairly seen as a liability in the workplace, due to common misconceptions and factors that are outside of our control. We are not less productive and not a liability. When that disability is hidden it becomes more complicated as your difficulties are often disregarded as "not that bad". I am more than happy to answer questions about my dyspraxia because I know it is so commonly misunderstood. I always explain my dyspraxia doesn't affect my work ethic. Many people have been keen to correct me by saying, "You mean dyslexia", and I often have to explain that while they may sound similar and share a couple of common traits, they are very different conditions that require different approaches.

Employers need to understand that neurodivergent individuals may not shine in a traditional interview setting because it requires thinking on your feet. A combination of nerves, probable tiredness, and stress mean that many are more likely to forget the answers under stress even though we are perfectly capable. I almost always never sleep the night before or eat before an interview, because I am too nervous. I always take notes with me, because it helps me remember the points I want to get across. I pick apart the job spec, and write it down along with examples. Otherwise, I can forget the question mid-way through answering.

I have repeatedly asked for interview questions in advance, and this has never been accommodated. I don't know if this is because it is misconstrued as a "step up" or an attempt to gain an advantage. The only reason I ask for questions in advance is to attempt to quell my anxiety. The guaranteed interview scheme is, in my view, a misguided attempt by employers to give a fair chance to neurodivergent individuals. But it often has the opposite effect because, even though they know you have a disability, an interview isn't tailored to cater towards your specific needs. Just because someone is neurodivergent doesn't mean that they will all have the same needs as each other. For example, I as someone who has dyspraxia prefer written communication to help me remember what has been said. I'm sure my dyslexic best friend couldn't imagine anything worse. To me, interviews always seem to be rushed and this increases my anxiety and stress levels, and means I'm less likely to get my points across as effectively as I would have liked. Most companies don't consider the specifics of employing neurodivergent talent, but they need to do this if they are serious about being a truly inclusive employer. Our support needs don't end after an interview. It is an ongoing need, and many employers fail to understand that we won't have a disability just because we have been working for them for a certain amount of time. Many employers don't seem to grasp that our disability won't simply magically stop affecting our day-to-day life because we are doing the same things.

Stopping unfair judgements about people with dyspraxia

Because I am unable to work full time, I have been in receipt of disability benefits since I was 16 years old. Despite this, I still face regular scrutiny whenever it is deemed that I have been disabled long enough. At 20 years old, I faced a tribunal after a routine medical, as it had been decided that I wasn't disabled and was fit to work full time. This was despite the fact that my conversation with them had lasted less than 30 minutes, that they had never met me previously, and that they freely admitted that they didn't know what dyspraxia was. Coming from supposed medical professionals, it's safe to say that I got an unpleasant surprise. I was fuming that the people who were supposedly qualified to judge how able I was or wasn't didn't even bother to seek out even basic information about dyspraxia before they made a decision. My benefit was stopped because they decided I didn't have a disability, so we appealed the decision and ultimately overturned it. The irony was, it was mentioned in the decision letter that they were almost surprised that I was intelligent and articulate, and yet could still have a significant disability. This just shows the lack of understanding that still surrounds dyspraxia. I don't enjoy being on benefits. There is a common misconception that if you receive benefits, particularly disability benefits, that you have to look or act a certain way to be socially acceptable to some people.

Someone who is articulate and seems intelligent and who lives independently with no obvious physical limitations doesn't fit the narrative of disability that we are often fed by the media and wider society. I have been told to my face in the past that I'm a liar, and that I can't possibly be disabled. You are often asked leading questions, and questions with little context that have little to nothing to do with your particular disability, and it seems this is done for no reason other than that reduce the number of people on benefits – and those with invisible disabilities are easy targets. It frustrates me that invisible disability is still treated as less than visible disability, or worse, a trend that people jump on.

8
Concluding comments

Anxiety, excitement, and hope for the future!

As I near the end of this book, my anxiety is starting to become absurd. And while I know that it is illogical, it's not enough to stop it from happening. I worry that people will believe I'm exaggerating my disability, that I'm being dramatic, or simply that I'm not a very good writer. My dyspraxia has always made me feel like an imposter, like I'm neither normal enough nor disabled enough to identify with either.

I am hopeful that, in the future, our ever-increasing knowledge of neurodivergence will mean that children who are experiencing what I did as a child will be met with more understanding and empathy than I was, rather than be made to feel like they are wrongly programmed and don't belong. The future for neurodivergent individuals looks to be getting better all the time, thanks to a growing awareness of neurodivergence and understanding of the unique talents that we can bring to the table. This means in turn that parents and carers will have the much-needed support that my parents did not, and having people available with lived experience to answer the burning questions that for many years went unanswered.

Aside from my personal (sky-high) excitement that I will finally have my own published book, which still blows my mind, I hope that my experiences will help others to better understand what it's like to live with a mind that likes to often do the opposite of what it should. And that, despite all that, minds like mine are still vital to help us better understand the human experience.

Discussion topics

Below are some queries for the reader to carefully consider and respond to:

- What are some of the issues that can follow the unapproved disclosure of students' disabilities in educational settings?
- Why might some neurodivergent employees experience mobbing in the workplace, what forms might mobbing take, and what are some likely outcomes?
- What are some of the ways in which the challenges experienced by people with dyspraxia can be dismissed?
- If you were a Minister for Employment, what strategies would you implement to employ more people with dyspraxia in a timely manner?
- What are the benefits and challenges with the wearing of the sunflower lanyard by neurodivergent people?
- What are some of the risks that can accompany negative reporting about neurodivergence in the mass media?

References

Armstrong, T. (2012). *Neurodiversity in the Classroom: Strength-based Strategies to Help Students with Special Needs Succeed in School and Life*, ASCD., Alexandria, Virginia

Colley, M. (2006). *Living with Dyspraxia: A Guide for Adults with Developmental Dyspraxia*, revised edition, Jessica Kingsley Publishers, London UK.

Dyspraxia Foundation. (2020). *Driving with dyspraxia.* [Online]. Available at: https://dyspraxiafoundation.org.uk/wp-content/uploads/2016/10/Driving20Sheet2020Oct16.pdf [Accessed].

Dyspraxia Foundation. (2024). *What is dyspraxia?* [Online]. Available at: https://dyspraxiafoundation.org.uk/ [Accessed].

Government UK. (2022). *Disabled people.* [Online]. Available at: www.gov.uk/browse/disabilities [Accessed].

Hidden Disabilities Sunflower Scheme. (2024). *Our history.* [Online]. Available at: https://hdsunflower.com/au/insights/post/history [Accessed].

Kirby, P. (2023). Codifying Clumsiness: Tracing the Origins of Dyspraxia through a Transatlantic Constellation of Mobility (1866–1948). *Journal of Historical Geography*, 82, pp. 134–143.

Mellifont, D. (2019). Mental Health and Media: A Study Exploring How Stigma is Promoted and Challenged within National Newspaper Reporting on Neurodivergence in Australia. *Communicator, 54(4),pp.,* 29–52.

Mullai, E. (2019). Collaboration of Auxiliary Teachers with Subject Teachers for the Inclusion of Children in Mainstream Schools. *European Journal of Research and Reflection in Educational Sciences*, 7 (2) pp.1–7.

O'Dea, Á., Stanley, M., Coote, S. and Robinson, K. (2021). Children and Young People's Experiences of Living with Developmental Coordination Disorder/Dyspraxia: A Systematic Review and Meta-ethnography of Qualitative Research. *PLoS One*, 16(3), e0245738.

Oxford Specialist Tutors. (2018). *What to do when your child is diagnosed with dyspraxia.* [Online]. Available at: https://oxfords pecialisttutors.com/dyspraxia-diagnosis/ [Accessed].

Polman, P. and Parker, R. (2024). *Why businesses must stop disregarding people with disabilities.* [Online]. Available at: https:// time.com/6246262/businesses-must-be-inclusive/ [Accessed].

Suskind, D. (2020). *Are you being mobbed at work?* [Online]. Available at: www.psychologytoday.com/au/blog/bully-wise/ 202012/are-you-being-mobbed-at-work [Accessed].

The Brain Charity. (2023). *What is masking, what does it look like and how can it affect people?* [Online]. Available at: www.thebrain charity.org.uk/what-is-masking/ [Accessed].

Index